Benchmark and Unit Tests

Grade 6

HOUGHTON MIFFLIN HARCOURT

Contents

Reading and Analyzing Text

Read the passage "The Perfect Job" before answering Numbers 1 through 6.

The Perfect Job

What do you think is the perfect job? I used to think it was one that would make me rich or famous, or both, but I recently came to realize that the best occupation is one that suits an individual perfectly. I learned this from my Uncle Charles, whose job fits him like a glove.

Charles is an Animal Control Officer (ACO) for the municipality[1] of Hartford, the town where I live, too. My father says jokingly that his brother likes animals better than people, and I share my father's opinion. He says that even as a kid Charles had a reputation for rescuing stray dogs, helping wounded chickadees, and plucking stranded cats from high branches. Today Charles can be recognized by his fascinating facial hair—a curly beard and handlebar mustache. He's content to live alone, companioned by the various critters that pass through his care.

One April day, my teachers had a conference to attend, and since my folks both work, I had permission to spend the day with Uncle Charles. Soon after I arrived at his farmhouse, the phone rang and he switched on the speakerphone so I could hear his call. A woman was on the line. "There's an animal in the woods behind my house," the woman quavered, "and it's howling over and over. The noise kept me awake all last night. Oh, please come fetch the poor thing."

"Be right over," Charles replied, jotting down her address on an old envelope. We hopped into his old red pickup truck and took off.

The woman lived on Upton Road, a rutted country lane lined with immense pines that created a gloomy shade, even though it was midday. When we pulled into the driveway at a mailbox numbered 458, a petite woman emerged from a small house wearing work clothes, a cap for shade from the sun, and muddy boots. She directed us toward the woods but admitted she was disinclined to go with us. "I think it's just a dog, but I was bitten by a dog when I was a child," she explained, "and I just don't want to take a chance."

---

¹municipality: the governing body of a city or town

We tromped through the nettles and sumac behind the house till we found a path into the woods. Suddenly we heard a pitiful yowl. "Stand back," my uncle commanded. I stayed a short distance behind him, but kept craning my neck around my uncle's frame. As we got closer, I saw a long, low-slung dog wearing a faded purple collar; the metal ring that holds the tags hung empty. She was cowering close to the ground, clearly more afraid of us than we were of her. She had long droopy ears, and her eyes, too, were droopy. She looked miserable.

My uncle whispered, "It's okay, girl," and she trembled but let him clip a leash to her collar and lead her to the truck. When he opened the back door, she hopped right in.

As we drove, I spoke soothingly to the dog, and she seemed to grow more comfortable with us. Back in my uncle's kitchen, he scrunched some blankets into a bed for her and put down fresh water and a dish of kibble. She gobbled the food and slurped the water, then flopped on the blankets and closed her droopy eyes. My uncle clomped into the kitchen and booted up his old computer.

"LOST DOG HARTFORD BASSET," he typed into the search engine. The computer hummed through the slow dial-up process until the classified ads for the local newspaper appeared, and my uncle began to scroll. There it was, the third ad down: a lost basset hound with a purple collar from Sumner, a neighboring town.

He called the phone number immediately, and when a man answered, my uncle introduced himself and passed on the good news. "They've found Happy!" I heard the man call to someone else. "We'll be right over, okay?" After my uncle gave him directions, the man was in such a hurry to hang up that he dropped the phone three times!

It wasn't long before a red convertible squealed into the driveway and a father and his son emerged. When Happy saw them, there was certainly no doubt that this was her family. The son got down on his hands and knees, laughing, hugging, and letting Happy jump, slobber, squirm, and wag as much as she wanted.

"We don't know how to thank you," the father confided to my uncle, his voice cracking some. "We've been sick with worry, and I must admit we feared the worst." There were tears in his eyes, but my uncle was grinning.

In that moment I understood that my Uncle Charles had the perfect occupation.

Now answer Numbers 1 through 6 on your Answer Sheet. Base your answers on the passage "The Perfect Job."

1 Read this excerpt from the passage.

> **"There's an animal in the woods behind my house," the woman quavered, "and it's howling over and over. The noise kept me awake all last night. Oh, please come fetch the poor thing."**

The excerpt above reveals that the woman is

A. angry.

B. bashful.

C. distraught.

D. untroubled.

2 Read this sentence from the passage.

> **She directed us toward the woods but admitted she was disinclined to go with us.**

If the word *inclined* means "of a mind," what does *disinclined* mean in the sentence above?

F. most likely

G. not willing

H. without hesitation

I. able to be convinced

3 Read this dictionary entry.

> **frame** (freym) *noun*
>
> 1. a border or case for enclosing a picture
> 2. a rigid structure that surrounds or encloses something
> 3. a human body; physique
> 4. a pair of eyeglasses, not including the lenses

Read this sentence from the passage.

> **I stayed a short distance behind him, but kept craning my neck around my uncle's frame.**

Which meaning best fits the way the word *frame* is used in the sentence above?

A. meaning 1

B. meaning 2

C. meaning 3

D. meaning 4

4 Read this sentence from the passage.

> **As we got closer, I saw a long, low-slung dog wearing a faded purple collar; the metal ring that holds the tags hung empty.**

What effect does the repetition of the *l* sound in the phrase *long, low-slung* have in the sentence above?

F. It helps create an alarming mood in the scene.

G. It draws readers' attention to the dog's size and shape.

H. It helps to show that the dog has been lost for a long time.

I. It draws readers' attention to the sounds that the dog is making.

4

5 The reader can conclude that Happy's owners

  A. grew up in Hartford.

  B. like to drive fast cars.

  C. gave up on finding the dog.

  D. were desperate to find the dog.

6 What does the reader learn about Uncle Charles?

  F. He is unhappy.

  G. He has no children of his own.

  H. He enjoys the company of animals.

  I. He does not get along well with people.

Read the article "On the Move with Freddy Adu" before answering
Numbers 7 through 12.

On the Move with Freddy Adu

by Marty Kaminsky

The crowd in R.F.K. Stadium anxiously scans the sideline. As Washington's D.C. United soccer team takes on the Chicago Fire, excited fans are looking for Freddy Adu (uh-DOO). "Where's Freddy?" they call from their seats.

Finally, 16-year-old Freddy Adu pulls off his warm-up suit. The crowd roars. As Freddy jogs up and down the sideline, waiting to enter the game, the chants grow louder and louder: "Fred-dy, Fred-dy."

Two minutes into his shift, Freddy breaks a move: the step-over. His left foot comes over the top of the ball, then the outside of his foot pushes it in the opposite direction. The Chicago Fire defender stumbles, giving Freddy just enough space to drill a shot wide of the goalkeeper.

The crowd is on its feet, oohing and aahing at the near miss. Freddy does not score this time, but it is plain for all to see: there are many goals to come in the future of this American soccer phenomenon[1].

At the age of 14, when most kids are starting eighth or ninth grade, Freddy signed the largest contract ever with Major League Soccer, the American men's professional league. A flood of stories about him immediately appeared in magazines and newspapers.

"It's pretty hard not to get caught up in all of it," Freddy admits. "But my friends and family remind me of what is most important and keep me grounded."

In 1997, Freddy's family moved from Ghana, West Africa, to Mrs. Adu's brother's house in the United States so that Freddy and his brother, Fro, could get a better education.

Freddy now lives with his mother and brother in Rockville, Maryland, not far from the home field of his team, D.C. United.

Although most sports stars hire assistants to handle their household chores, Freddy's mom treats Freddy like any other 16-year-old. "My mom makes me do chores, like the dishes, same as before," Freddy laments. "I don't like it, but I do it."

In Ghana, kids were constantly knocking on Freddy's door to ask him to play soccer. From age two on, Freddy played barefoot games on sandy fields.

[1]**phenomenon:** a remarkable person or thing

"I did not go one day without soccer," Freddy recalls. "There were no coaches, so it was just kicking and learning on your own."

As he got older, Freddy began playing in games with boys twice his age and in scrimmages against men.

Soon after arriving in America at the age of eight, Freddy was discovered by a schoolmate's dad, a youth-soccer coach. Freddy joined the coach's all-star team.

When Freddy was 10, the team traveled to an international tournament in Italy, where Freddy scored four goals in five games and won the Most Valuable Player award. An Italian professional league offered Freddy a contract at that time, but Mrs. Adu turned it down. Freddy explains, "I was only 10. . . . As usual, she was looking out for my well-being in the long run."

When Freddy returned to the United States, Mrs. Adu let him attend a sports boarding school in Florida that is run by the U.S. Soccer Federation. Freddy completed all his course requirements and finished high school when he was 14.

By then, Freddy had drawn the interest of some of the soccer world's most important people. Bruce Arena, coach of the USA men's national team, noted, "He's strong, he's quick, he's agile. He's got good balance, and he's got great vision. . . . This player may be our first superstar."

Although teams from around the world clamored for Freddy's attention, Freddy decided to play in the United States. He wanted to live as normal a teenage life as possible. "I like to do lots of things that other teenagers do," Freddy says. "One of the hardest things for me is that soccer is my work, so I don't have a normal teenage life. I travel around a lot and hang out with guys much older than me who have different interests."

It might be easy for a 16-year-old to let it go to his head when fans chant his name and beg for autographs, but Freddy has learned a lot in his two years with D.C. United. "I am just one person on a team—I'm not the whole team," he explains. "And this is about more than soccer—it is about how you carry yourself, how you behave, and how much you respect others."

Name _____ Date _____

Now answer Numbers 7 through 12 on your Answer Sheet. Base your answers on the article "On the Move with Freddy Adu."

7   At the beginning of the article, why does the author describe the opening minutes of a soccer game between Washington's D.C. United and the Chicago Fire?

    A.   to demonstrate Freddy Adu's skill and talent

    B.   to explain how competitive the two teams are

    C.   to illustrate why footwork is so important in soccer

    D.   to show why Freddy Adu joined D.C. United's team

8   Read this sentence from the article.

> **The Chicago Fire defender stumbles, giving Freddy just enough space
> to drill a shot wide of the goalkeeper.**

    What does the word *defender* mean in the sentence above?

    F.   someone who observes an athletic event

    G.   someone whose primary duty is to attempt to score

    H.   someone responsible for directing or training athletes

    I.   someone responsible for guarding an opposing player

9   Read this sentence from the article

> **Freddy does not score this time, but it is plain for all to see: there are
> many goals to come in the future of this American soccer phenomenon.**

    Which sentence below uses the word *plain* in the same way as in
the sentence above?

    A.   The boy's face seemed plain—until he smiled broadly.

    B.   My mother's meaning was very plain: homework comes first.

    C.   The doctor suggested I eat a plain diet as I recovered from the flu.

    D.   For her interview, she picked out a plain black skirt and white blouse.

Name _____ Date _____

10 The author's attitude toward Freddy Adu is

    F. admiring.

    G. concerned.

    H. fanatical.

    I. skeptical.

11 Read this sentence from the article

> **A flood of stories about him immediately appeared in magazines and newspapers.**

What does the author mean by the phrase *a flood* as used in the sentence above?

    A. a large number in quick succession

    B. a subject or topic of great importance

    C. a collection or body of work written by one person

    D. something written in a rushed and often careless way

12 Which of the author's statements about Freddy Adu is an opinion?

    F. "In 1997, Freddy's family moved from Ghana, West Africa, to Mrs. Adu's brother's house in the United States. . . ."

    G. "An Italian professional league offered Freddy a contract at that time, but Mrs. Adu turned it down."

    H. "Although teams from around the world clamored for Freddy's attention, Freddy decided to play in the United States."

    I. "It might be easy for a 16-year-old to let it go to his head when fans chant his name and beg for autographs . . . ."

Read the article "Everything You Wanted to Know About Pencils" before answering Numbers 13 through 17.

Everything You Wanted To Know About Pencils

The story of pencils begins about 500 years ago in the Cumberland Hills of England. One day, after a violent storm, a group of shepherds went out to check their sheep and saw that several trees had blown over, exposing a grey-black glistening substance. Like coal, it quickly stained their fingers, but unlike coal, it would not burn. They did, however, discover that the new substance was excellent for marking the sheep! They called the substance black lead.

Eventually, someone developed a holder for black lead. A piece of wood was hollowed out and a piece of black lead was placed inside. The wood could then be scraped away as the writing material was used. Later, people started using a different method to make pencils. Two pieces of planed and smoothed wood were glued around a narrow stick of black lead. This technique is still used today. About the same time, a Swedish chemist learned that black lead, like its upscale cousin, the diamond, was a form of carbon. He renamed black lead *graphite*, which comes from a Greek word meaning "to write."

In the early nineteenth century, most pencils sold in the United States were imported from Europe. Soon, however, pencil factories started to open. Early pencils were unpainted, to show off their high quality wood. Most pencils were made from Eastern Red Cedar, a strong splinter-resistant wood that grows in the eastern United States.

As more and more pencils were made and sold, competition became strong and advertising became essential. The biggest and best pencil makers painted their pencils yellow to show that they used Chinese graphite, the finest in the world. In China, yellow is the color of royalty and respect, so pencil makers chose yellow for their highest-quality products. Today, seventy-five percent of the pencils sold in the United States are yellow.

Today's pencils are made with more than just graphite. Graphite is combined with clay and inserted into a wooden casing. This combination will probably be used throughout the next centuries.

Pencil Facts

- Most pencils are hexagonal, which is comfortable to hold, and it means the pencils won't roll off desks.

- Pencils work in space because they do not use gravity, unlike most pens.

- Most U.S. pencils have erasers, but most European pencils do not.

- A typical pencil can write 45,000 words.

- A typical pencil can draw a line 35 miles long!

- Pencils are labeled according to the hardness of their graphite. In the United States, a #2 is medium, which is preferred during standardized tests.

Now answer Numbers 13 through 17 on your Answer Sheet. Base your answers on the article "Everything You Wanted to Know About Pencils."

13 What purpose does the anecdote about the shepherds in the first paragraph serve in the overall article?

A. It shows how black lead first came to the United States.

B. It demonstrates how the substance black lead is formed.

C. It introduces the idea of how black lead was first discovered and used.

D. It illustrates the importance of pencils in some of the earliest societies.

14 What was most likely the author's purpose for writing this article?

F. to compare and contrast different types of pencils

G. to explain the history behind how pencils are made

H. to describe the process by which all pencils are made

I. to tell about interesting ways that pencils can be used

15 Read this excerpt from the article.

> **Eventually, someone developed a holder for black lead. A piece of wood
> was hollowed out and a piece of black lead was placed inside. The wood
> could then be scraped away as the writing material was used. Later,
> people started using a different method to make pencils. Two pieces of
> planed and smoothed wood were glued around a narrow stick of black
> lead. This technique is still used today.**

Which of the following best describes how the text structure of this excerpt
contributes to the development of the author's central idea?

A. The author uses problem-solution to show how pencils made writing simpler
and neater.

B. The author uses a sequence of events to help readers understand how pencil-
making has changed.

C. The author uses comparison-contrast to help readers distinguish between
black lead and graphite.

D. The author uses cause-and-effect to show why people began gluing wood
around black lead to make pencils.

16 Read this sentence from the article.

> **About the same time, a Swedish chemist learned that black lead, like
> its upscale cousin, the diamond, was a form of carbon.**

What does the word *chemist* mean in the sentence above?

F. the study of chemistry

G. a substance produced in chemistry

H. relating to or concerned with chemistry

I. a scientist who specializes in chemistry

17 Read this sentence from the article.

> **In the early nineteenth century, most pencils sold in the United States
> were imported from Europe.**

What does the word *imported* mean in the sentence above?

A. introduced for the first time

B. transported by ship or other means

C. brought into a country from abroad

D. made or processed into a finished product

Read the poem "California Beach" before answering Numbers 18 through 23.

California Beach

I.

Horns honk in smoggy rush hour traffic.
A big man hoses down a sidewalk,
while another empties trash cans from the day before.
Early morning joggers pant, sweat, stare.
Seagulls scavenge yesterday's fries as moms push babies in strollers,
and somewhere a boom box thumps
as the sky turns from rosy pink to orange to yellow to red to turquoise,
thick and perfect as paint.
The waves lick the sand gently as the tide and the people flow in.

II.

People on blankets soak up sun, while
the smell of coconut oil plays hide and seek with your nose.
Artists sell watercolors of the wooden pier
while surfers wait in the doldrums for waves,
toddlers wail, sleepy, and couples walk hand in hand.
A steel drum clangs and teenagers dance,
seagulls beg for potato chips,
the sun rises high.
"Burritos!" shouts a vendor.
Inline skates, bicycles, skateboards, scooters.
"Wait up!" yells a girl on a pink tricycle.
The tide retreats, leaving the clamor[1] behind.

[1]**clamor:** loud sustained noise

III.

Palm trees are silhouettes against fire as the sun sinks.
Families giggle, chasing beach balls in the sand
as old men play chess in the shade.
Artists pack their wares, bid goodnight, and depart,
and seagulls dine on pizza crusts as seaweed dries, clouds drift, breezes
whisper, break-dancers spin. Children swing so high
their sandals touch the violet clouds, the sun
now an ember, glowing red, pink, then purple.
The tide rises, always moving,
always changing, always the same.

Name _____ Date _____

Now answer Numbers 18 through 23 on your Answer Sheet. Base your answers on the poem "California Beach."

18 Read these lines from the poem.

> **as the sky turns from rosy pink to orange to yellow to red to
> turquoise, / thick and perfect as paint.**

In the line above, the author compares the colors of the sky to paint to show

   F. that morning has arrived.

   G. how brilliant the colors are.

   H. how nice the weather will be.

   I. that the sun's rays are intense.

19 Read this line from the poem.

> **the smell of coconut oil plays hide and seek with your nose.**

In the line above, the author says *the smell of coconut oil plays hide and seek with your nose* to

   A. show that the coconut oil's scent comes and goes.

   B. show that the coconut oil's scent is overwhelming.

   C. imply that the scent of coconut oil is difficult to describe.

   D. show how quickly the scent of coconut oil moves through the air.

20 Which detail from the third verse shows that evening is approaching?

   F. clouds drift

   G. old men play chess

   H. the sun/now an ember

   I. seagulls dine on pizza crusts

Name _____ Date _____

21 One way the poet marks the passing of time is by

    A. showing the rise and fall of the tide.

    B. referring to the noises heard at midday.

    C. contrasting dark trees against the sunset.

    D. describing people of many different ages.

22 Read this line from the poem.

    Artists pack their wares, bid goodnight, and depart,

What does the word *depart* mean in the sentence above?

    F. draw

    G. leave

    H. share

    I. speak

23 Which word best describes the poem's overall tone?

    A. determined

    B. humorous

    C. lively

    D. sad

Read the passage "'Evacuate!'" before answering Numbers 24 through 29.

"Evacuate!"

Emil and his family live thirty-five kilometers north of Mount Merapi, an active volcano in Central Java in Indonesia, on land that his great-great-great-grandparents once farmed. They are as firmly planted there as the rice that returns every year to their fields.

For weeks now, the family has heard Merapi, which means mountain of fire, rumbling and grumbling like an underground giant. Lava flows down the north side of Mount Merapi. Hot ash and steam spew from the top. Already, gas clouds have nearly choked one village, and ash has covered another with a thick, gray blanket.

"This morning we raised the status of Merapi to red, which is the top alert," said the head of the Center for Vulcanologic Research. "Since the mountain is in a state of constant lava flow, every resident within forty kilometers has been ordered to evacuate."

After their evening meal of nasi goreng, a traditional meal of rice, egg, and chicken, Emil's father and uncle sit and discuss the news. Usually, Emil would go with his brother and two sisters to play badminton outside. Tonight, he wants to hear what the men say, so he crouches behind a chair to avoid notice.

Emil's father is a tall, thin man with a soft voice. He sits on one side of the room and calmly explains that they must stay. He argues that all they own in both houses, including the livestock, will be in danger, not just from the volcano but also from looters. He says that the crops might be saved if they stay, but they will certainly die if the family leaves. Without the crops, he says, the two families will have nothing to eat when they return. Emil's father reminds his brother that the government has evacuated the people before and the lava did not reach them.

His older brother, a big man with a huge black beard and a gruff voice, answers that they must leave. The military trucks will come and make them leave. He says the military has had to use force in some of the villages, and his voice cracks as he talks. "Every time the mountain erupts, people suffer," he says, "and it is always the foolish people who decide to stay."

Emil can see his father tremble as he looks out at the rice paddies he has tended since he was a boy. Suddenly, he notices his son crouching behind the chair. "Go outside and play with the others," he barks. Emil obeys him, as he always does.

The next morning, the children rise to find that all the families' belongings have been packed. In the distance, Merapi moans and groans, and the sky to the south is dark with ash and smoke. After the chores are complete, the two families will head north.

Now answer Numbers 24 through 29 on your Answer Sheet. Base your answers on the passage "'Evacuate!'"

 24 Which statement best describes Emil's point of view in the passage?

   F. Emil is an unconcerned observer.

   G. Emil is the narrator of the passage.

   H. Emil directs the events of the passage.

   I. Emil is both a participant and an observer.

25 Read this dictionary entry.

> **state** (steyt) *noun*
> 1. the condition of something
> 2. social position or rank
> 3. a nation or politically organized society
> 4. the activities of a central, civil government

Read this sentence from the passage.

> **"Since the mountain is in a state of constant lava flow, every resident within forty kilometers has been ordered to evacuate."**

Which meaning best fits the way the word *state* is used in the sentence above?

A. meaning 1

B. meaning 2

C. meaning 3

D. meaning 4

26 Mount Merapi symbolizes

F. the islands of Indonesia.

G. volcanoes around the world.

H. the end of the harvest season.

I. the unpredictable force of nature.

27 What is Emil's father's argument for staying?

A. The volcano is far away, and it is only posing a risk to towns and villages.

B. The families must remain at home to look after their animals and crops, and they should never give in to the government.

C. If the families leave, they will risk losing their animals and crops; and, at any rate, the government has unnecessarily evacuated people before.

D. If the families leave, they will certainly die, as there will be nothing to eat when they return; and, at any rate, the government is not always right.

Name _____ Date _____

28 Read this sentence from the passage.

> "Every time the mountain erupts, people suffer," he says, "and it is always the foolish people who decide to stay."

What does the sentence above best reveal about Emil's uncle's in the passage?

F. He is fearful of staying.

G. He is undecided about leaving.

H. He is respectful of Emil's father.

I. He is angry with the government.

29 The overall tone of this passage can best be described as

A. casual.

B. lighthearted.

C. somber.

D. surprising.

Read the article "Spend or Save!" before answering Numbers 30 through 35.

Spend or Save!

Many people are paid either weekly or monthly, because they have a job, or because they get an allowance. These people have expenses, too, or things that cost them money. The earned money can help them take care of those expenses.

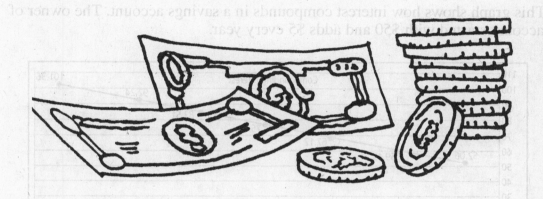

The Choice

One person may choose to spend the money he or she earns immediately. This person may purchase triple-fudge brownies, newly released video games, or perhaps tickets to a popular movie. Soon this person may be out of funds, having spent all that hard-earned money. A different person may choose not to spend the money right away, but save it, stashing the money under his or her mattress or investing it in a bank.

Why Save?

Saving is actually easy to do, especially if the money is deposited into a savings account. The savings account is kept by the bank, and the money in the account earns interest. Interest is earned based on the amount of money in the account. This is called the balance. An interest rate of three percent earns three cents for every dollar kept in the account. The longer the money is kept in the account, the more interest that is earned. Interest is added to the existing balance. Soon the interest becomes part of a new balance and earns interest. This phenomenon is called compound interest. Money left for long periods of time in a bank earns money, almost as though it gets its own allowance!

How to Save

There are several ways to increase the amount of money available to put in the bank. One is to take an amount of money from a paycheck or allowance and transfer it immediately to the bank, before spending any money. The second is to create a plan, or budget, by keeping a money diary, writing down all the money earned and all the money spent on expenses. Looking at the diary can help determine which expenses are necessary and which might not be. Once all of the necessary expenses have been calculated, the money left over could be deposited in a savings account. Another way to save is to cut expenses by shopping for sales or going to matinee[1] movies instead of the more expensive evening shows.

Whether a person is a spender or saver, there are many ways to cut expenses and to save. And because money kept in a savings account continues to grow, it is beneficial to put as much in the account as soon as possible.

This graph shows how interest compounds in a savings account. The owner of the account started with $50 and adds $5 every year.

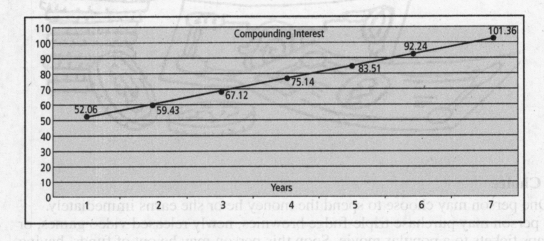

Now answer Numbers 30 through 35 on your Answer Sheet. Base your answers on the article "Spend or Save!"

30 The purpose of this article is to

   F. encourage readers to save money.

   G. entertain readers with stories about money.

   H. give information about interest rates at various banks.

   I. explain how savings and checking accounts are different.

[1]**matinee:** a daytime theater performance or movie showing

Name _____   Date _____

31 Read this sentence from the article.

> **A different person may choose not to spend the money right away, but save it, stashing the money under his or her mattress, or investing it in a bank.**

What does the word *investing* mean in the sentence above?

A. presenting money as a donation

B. concealing money in a safe place

C. putting money to use in order to gain more back

D. dividing money amongst several people or groups

32 From the author's point of view, what is the primary reason a person should deposit money into a savings account?

F. Your money will earn interest.

G. The bank will help you create a budget.

H. The bank will keep you updated on your existing balance.

I. It will prevent you from spending the money you earn immediately.

33 Read this sentence from the article.

> **One is to take an amount of money from a paycheck or allowance and transfer it immediately to the bank, before spending any money.**

What does the word *transfer* mean in the sentence above?

A. borrow

B. increase

C. lend

D. move

Name _____ Date _____

34 How does the author support the claim that keeping a money diary can help people increase the amount of money they have available to put in the bank?

    F. It can help them to earn more allowance or find a higher-paying job.

    G. It can help them determine and then cut back on unnecessary expenses.

    H. It can convince them to put all of their money in the bank rather than spend it.

    I. It can show them how much interest they will earn by putting money in the bank.

35 Using the information in the article and the graph, how much money will the owner of the account have after five years?

    A. $0

    B. $5.00

    C. $67.12

    D. $83.51

Revising and Editing

Read the introduction and the article "The American Museum of Natural History" before answering Numbers 1 through 7.

Melissa wrote this article about the American Museum of Natural History. Read her article and think about the changes she should make.

The American Museum of Natural History

(1) If you go to New York City, plan on visiting the American Museum of Natural History. (2) You may have seen the museum in a popular fictional movie about what happens to the exhibits at night. (3) As exciting as the museum looks in the movie, it is even more exciting in real life.

(4) To enter the museum, you walk up several concrete stairs. (5) When you step inside, a very, very big, long-necked dinosaur skeleton greets you. (6) Just ahead are 28 mammal dioramas featuring a herd of life-sized elephants and other African mammals.

(7) Go down a level to the first floor and you will find a 94-foot-long blue whale in the Milstein Hall of Ocean Life. (8) This amazing cite is suspended from the ceiling high above you. (9) In this big Hall, visitors admire not only the blue whale, but also marine animals and plants of all shapes and sizes.

(10) The Arthur Ross Hall of Meteorites is also located on the first floor. (11) Here you will find moon rocks. (12) You will find other interesting items from space, including the Cape York Meteorite, the world's largest meteorite in a museum. (13) It weighs an astounding 34 tons. (14) If you enjoy learning about space, be sure to visit the museum's Rose Center for Earth

Name _____ Date _____

and Space. (15) It is home to a planetarium and numerous exhibits about

the stars and planets.

(16) The museum is open almost every day from 10 A.M.

to 5:45 P.M. (17) There is so much to see, do, and learn at the museum

a knowledgeable tour guide can help you discover all the museum

has to offer.

Now answer Numbers 1 through 7 on your Answer Sheet. Base your answers on the changes Melissa should make.

1 What change should be made in sentence 5?

   A. delete the comma after *inside*

   B. change *very, very big* to **gigantic**

   C. change *dinosaur* to **Dinosaur**

   D. change *greets* to **greeted**

2 Which sentence could best follow sentence 6?

   F. The elephant is the largest living land mammal.

   G. Each year, millions of people visit the museum.

   H. They are so life-like that you can practically smell them!

   I. The American Museum of Natural History has changing exhibits.

3 What change should be made in sentence 8?

   A. change *amazing* to **amazed**

   B. change *cite* to **sight**

   C. change *suspended* to **suspends**

   D. insert a comma after *above*

4 What change should be made in sentence 9?

F. change *Hall* to **hall**

G. delete the comma after *whale*

H. change *marine* to **Marine**

I. change the period to a question mark

5 What is the best way to combine sentences 11 and 12?

A. Here you will find moon rocks and other interesting items from space, including the Cape York Meteorite, the world's largest meteorite in a museum.

B. Here you will find moon rocks and other interesting items from space, it is the world's largest meteorite in a museum including the Cape York Meteorite.

C. Here you will find moon rocks and you will find other interesting items from space, including the Cape York Meteorite, the world's largest meteorite in a museum.

D. Here you will find moon rocks and items from space that are interesting, including you will find the Cape York Meteorite, the world's largest meteorite in a museum.

6 What change should be made in sentence 13?

F. change *It* to **Its**

G. change *weighs* to **ways**

H. change *tons* to **ton**

I. change the period to an exclamation point

7 What is the best way to revise sentence 17?

A. There is so much to see, do, and learn at the museum a knowledgeable tour guide can help you discover.

B. There is so much to see, do, and learn at the museum a knowledgeable tour guide. Can help you discover all the museum has to offer.

C. There is so much to see, do, and learn at the museum. A knowledgeable tour guide can help you discover all the museum has to offer.

D. There is so much to see, do, and learn at the museum because a knowledgeable tour guide can help you discover all the museum has to offer.

Read the introduction and the passage "Testing the Water" before answering Numbers 8 through 14.

Evan wrote a passage about how he overcame a fear. Read his passage and think about the changes he should make.

Testing the Water

(1) Many people are afraid of something. (2) For example, they might have a phobia of big spiders or chaotic thunderstorms. (3) These specific fears do not apply to me. (4) I have a pet tarantula named "Buddy," and I happen to enjoy a sudden flash of lightning and an earsplitting clap of thunder. (5) However, I did have one fear. (6) As ridiculous as it might sound, throughout my entire life I've been absolutely terrified of water.

(7) My friends enjoy swimming. (8) Most members of my family enjoy swimming. (9) On Saturdayes, whenever the weather got warm, my friends and family members would try to get me to swim at the local swimming pool with them. (10) Of course, I always had some excuse about why I couldn't go, and sometimes I refused their invitations outright. (11) I usually regretted this decision, but what else could I do.

(12) This summer I signed up for swimming lessons at the Kilgore Community center. (13) I've done so each summer in the past, but I always cancelled at the last minute. (14) This year I forced myself to show up on the first day.

(15) Fortunately, I had a well-trained instructor. (16) Patient and understanding. (17) My teacher knew just what to say and how far to nudge me before I became uncomfortable. (18) By the end of the first day, I was already submerging my face in the water. (19) By the end of the week, I was actually swimming!

Name _____ Date _____

(20) Now my friends and family do not have to coxe me to go to

the pool with them. (21) I'm usually the one trying to get them to go.

(22) I am also the first one in the water!

_____

Now answer Numbers 8 through 14 on your Answer Sheet. Base your answers on the changes Evan should make.

8 What is the best way to combine sentences 7 and 8?

   F. My friends and most members of my family enjoy swimming.

   G. My friends enjoy swimming and my family members enjoy swimming most.

   H. My friends enjoy swimming most members of my family enjoy swimming, too.

   I. My friends enjoy swimming and members of my family mostly enjoy swimming, too.

9 What change should be made in sentence 9?

   A. change *Saturdayes* to **Saturdays**

   B. delete the comma after *warm*

   C. change *swim* to **swims**

   D. change *local swimming pool* to **Local Swimming Pool**

10 What change should be made in sentence 11?

   F. change *regretted* to **regret**

   G. change *decision* to **decisions**

   H. change *do* to **did**

   I. change the period to a question mark

11 What change should be made in sentence 12?

   A. change *signed* to **sign**

   B. change *lessons* to **lessones**

   C. change *center* to **Center**

   D. change the period to a question mark

12 Which sentence could best be added after sentence 14?

   F. Swimming looks like a lot of fun, but it frightens me.

   G. My older brother learned to swim at the community center.

   H. Swimming lessons are offered in sessions that run for four weeks.

   I. I was so nervous that my heart was racing and my palms were sweating.

13 What is the best way to combine sentences 16 and 17?

   A. My teacher, patient and understanding, knew just what to say and how far to nudge me before I became uncomfortable.

   B. Patient and understanding my teacher knew just what to say, and how far to nudge me, before I became uncomfortable.

   C. Before I became uncomfortable, my teacher became patient and understanding, knowing just what to say and how far to nudge.

   D. Patient and understanding, knowing just what to say and how far to nudge me before I became uncomfortable was my teacher.

14 What change should be made in sentence 20?

   F. insert a comma after *family*

   G. change *coxe* to **coax**

   H. change *go* to **goes**

   I. change *pool* to **Pool**

Read the introduction and the article "A Book Worth Reading" before answering Numbers 15 through 20.

Kenzie wrote this article about a book she read. Read her article and think about the changes she should make.

A Book Worth Reading

(1) The writer Avery Fisher has done it again? (2) You will want to read her latest book, *On the Job,* over and over. (3) In it, twelve-year-old Meagan devotes a weekend to babysitting classes to learn the ins and outs of caring for children. (4) By the end of the following week, her neighbor hires her to go with the family on a camping trip and help the mother with her three young childrens.

(5) The camping trip begins well, and Meagan is enjoying herself and her job. (6) On a walk in the woods with the family, Meagans' relaxation vanishes when the two-year old falls down and gets a cut. (7) At first, Meagan panics, but she quickly recovers and remembers her training. (8) She takes the first aid kit out of her backpack, puts on gloves, and begins cleansing the cut and covering it with a bandage while the mother watches.

(9) Readers will enjoy the action in the book. (10) They will sympathize with the struggles Meagan faces. (11) Readers will sympathize with the struggles Meagan overcomes. (12) Young babysitters will realize that the job involves more than just entertaining it is a lot of work and responsibility.

(13) With her latest book, Avery Fisher sends a message in a great, great way!

Now answer Numbers 15 through 20 on your Answer Sheet. Base your answers on the changes Kenzie should make.

15 What change should be made in sentence 1?

    A. change *writer* to **Writer**

    B. insert a comma after *Fisher*

    C. change *has* to **had**

    D. change the question mark to an exclamation point

16 What change should be made in sentence 4?

    F. delete the comma after *week*

    G. change *hires* to **hired**

    H. change *mother* to **Mother**

    I. change *childrens* to **children**

17 What change should be made in sentence 6?

    A. change *Meagans'* to **Meagan's**

    B. change *vanishes* to **vanyshes**

    C. insert a period after *down*

    D. change *gets* to **got**

18 What is the best way to combine sentences 10 and 11?

    F. They will sympathize with the struggles Meagan faces and overcomes.

    G. They will sympathize with the struggles and overcomes Meagan faces.

    H. They will sympathize with the struggles she overcomes and Meagan faces.

    I. They will sympathize with Meagan and struggles and readers will sympathize with the struggles she overcomes.

19 What is the best way to rewrite the ideas in sentence 12?

  A. Young babysitters will realize that the job involves more than just entertaining, work, and responsibility.

  B. Young babysitters will realize that the job involves more than just entertaining. A lot of work and responsibility.

  C. Young babysitters will realize. The job involves more than just entertaining it is a lot of work and responsibility.

  D. Young babysitters will realize that the job involves more than just entertaining. It is a lot of work and responsibility.

20 What change should be made in sentence 13?

  F. change *book* to **Book**

  G. change *sends* to **sent**

  H. insert a comma after *message*

  I. change *great, great* to **wonderful**

Name _____ Date _____

Writing to Narrate

Read the prompt and plan your response.

> Most people have overcome a challenge in their life.
>
> Think about a challenge that a character might have to overcome.
>
> Now write a story about a character who overcomes a challenge.

Planning Page

Use this space to make your notes before you begin writing. The writing on this page will NOT be scored.

_____

_____

_____

_____

_____

_____

_____

_____

_____

_____

_____

_____

_____

Name _____ Date _____

Begin writing your response here. The writing on this page and the next page
WILL be scored.

_____

_____

_____

_____

_____

_____

_____

_____

_____

_____

_____

_____

_____

_____

_____

_____

_____

_____

_____

_____

_____

_____

_____

_____

_____

Name _____ Date _____

_____

_____

_____

_____

_____

_____

_____

_____

_____

_____

_____

_____

_____

_____

_____

_____

_____

_____

_____

_____

_____

_____

_____

_____

Reading Complex Text

Read the article "The Great Race for Mercy." As you read, stop and answer each question. Use evidence from the article to support your answers.

The Great Race for Mercy

It is March. The streets of downtown Anchorage are teeming with spectators, media, and fans, all buzzing with anticipation. No one feels this anticipation more keenly than the sled dogs and drivers preparing to compete in one of the world's most challenging races: the Iditarod Trail Sled Dog Race. The race begins in Anchorage and sends competitors approximately 1,100 miles over Alaska's rugged terrain to Nome, Alaska. To beat out the competition, a team must skillfully overcome harsh winds along the Yukon River, mountain storms, shifting ice on the Norton Sound, and freezing temperatures—not to mention fatigue, self-doubt, and injury. At the end of the race, one musher and his or her team of dogs are crowned champion. Needless to say, Iditarod competitors are famed for their strength, endurance, and determination.

Remarkably, the Iditarod trail was once the site of great teamwork rather than competition. Part of the trail was used by several teams of mushers and dogs who worked together to save the children of the small town of Nome, in an effort remembered as "The Great Race for Mercy."

---

1 How does the author's focus on competition in the first paragraph contrast with the ideas in the second paragraph?

_____

_____

_____

In January 1925, the town of Nome, Alaska, was facing the onset of an epidemic of the disease diphtheria that threatened the entire population. Most at risk were Nome's children. The few medical professionals in Nome determined that the only way to stop the disease from spreading was to obtain enough serum to treat those who had fallen ill. The serum was located in Anchorage, nearly 1,000 miles away. It was transported 350 miles by train to Nenana. There, the journey was forced to a halt. The railroad tracks went no further. From Nenana, there were few options. The airplanes that carried passengers and supplies from Nenana to Nome in summer remained grounded in winter. The only solution was the old Iditarod Trail dogsled route. Developed in the early 1900s, this path was used by mining companies and their dogsled teams.

With no time to waste, the lives of Nome's children were put in the hands of Alaska's best mushers and their dogs.

> **2** What are two words or phrases from the section above that help you understand the meaning of the word *epidemic*?
>
> _____
>
> _____
>
> _____

Mushers throughout Alaska quickly came together to deliver the serum to Nome as soon as possible. Communicating by telegraph, the mushers set up a system to relay the serum from one dogsled team to the next. The first team would meet the train in Nenana, where they would pick up the crate of serum. Then, they would race to the first transfer point along the route to meet the next team. Typically, it took a solid month for a dogsled team to travel from Nenana to Nome. If the relay worked as planned, fresh dogsled teams would be ready and waiting at each point at a moment's notice. The serum just might reach Nome in less than two weeks. Even then, would it be too late?

The conditions in Alaska in January made even travel by dogsled dangerous. Temperatures ranged between 40 and 70 degrees below zero. Winds constantly pounded the mushers and their dogs. But the teams bravely carried on, despite enormous risks to both man and dog.

One of the most famous legs of the trip occurred as the serum neared Nome. With the epidemic claiming lives daily, the sense of urgency was at a peak among the mushers and their dogs. Musher Leonard Seppala and his lead dog Togo had traveled miles from Nome, crossing the treacherous ice flows of the Norton Sound. As the team approached the town of Shaktoolik, they encountered another musher heading in their direction with the serum. Seppala promptly loaded the crate onto his sled, turned around, and traveled back in the direction of Nome. Crossing the Norton Sound once again, the unthinkable happened. Seppala's dogs broke through the ice and fell into the freezing water. Following Togo's example, the other dogs remained calm as Seppala, in a heroic act, pulled them to safety. After treating his dogs' paws, Seppala and his team pushed onward. Before the serum reached its final destination, however, another near-disaster would occur. And another dog would rise to the occasion and become a hero.

In the town of Bluff, an Alaskan husky named Balto was waiting patiently for his team's turn to run. Musher Gunnar Kaasen trusted Balto, but Balto did not have much experience as a lead dog. When Kaasen's team finally had secured the serum, Kaasen harnessed his dogs, placing Balto toward the rear. The team set off for Port Safety, where the final team awaited. Unknown to Kaasen, the coastal route between the towns of Bluff and Port Safety was directly in the path of a raging blizzard.

Kaasen's team plowed ahead until the violent winds and blowing snow caused the lead dog to stop in its tracks. Unable to sense the trail, the dog refused to go on. From the back of the pack, Balto barked and whined. Balto was letting Kaasen know that he knew the way. Soon, the team was back on the trail. This time, a confident Balto took the lead. Balto's intuition was faultless. Not only could he sense the trail, he also sensed where trouble lay ahead and steered his team around unsafe ice. The town of Port Safety was dark when Kaasen and his team finally arrived. Instead of stopping, Kaasen urged Balto on toward the final destination. At dawn, Balto delivered his team and the precious serum to Nome.

3 Explain the role that Balto played in helping to deliver the serum to Nome.

_____

_____

_____

The entire journey from Nenana to Nome had taken less than six days, an extraordinary feat considering the conditions and coordination involved. Perhaps more extraordinary is the spirit in which this journey was undertaken and carried out by the mushers and their dogs. Their actions saved the lives of countless children of Nome. It is the spirit of this journey, and of Alaska's sled dog history, that inspired the Iditarod Trail Sled Dog Race.

4 First tell why the author wrote this article. Then explain how the author uses the stories about Togo and Balto to help convey this purpose.

_____

_____

_____

_____

Reading and Analyzing Text

Read the article "Kids Making a Difference" and the flyer "WANTED: Rock Stars and Role Models!" before answering Numbers 1 through 17.

Kids Making a Difference

All around the country, the power of older kids is making an impressive impact. These students are showing they have a valuable talent for inspiring younger children to do their best.

Tutors in Seattle

Young children sometimes become frustrated by their homework. In one Seattle after-school program, student tutors come to the rescue by making learning into a game that kids enjoy. They also read to the children and help them with crafts when their homework is done. The younger students are happy to get help with their homework, and they are even happier to get the attention of older students!

Adults in the program say the tutors are great role models. The student tutors say they get a great experience from working with kids. It gives them confidence and improves their communication skills while also giving them something fun and worthwhile to do after school.

Youth Coaches in Jacksonville

What's better than a play day at school? A play day with teen coaches! Just ask the six hundred students at a Florida elementary school. Each year, they spend a special day with dozens of high school athletes.

The teens teach all kinds of athletic skills. Some kids learn to slam-dunk a basketball, while others learn the fundamentals of tennis. The teen coaches also give pointers on passing a football, swinging a bat, and dribbling a soccer ball. Even more importantly, the athletes take time to explain how they balance sports and schoolwork. Chances are good their message gets through, too, because their star-struck young listeners hang on every word the teens say!

Salsa Teachers in Boston

When asked what they wished their children could do after school, parents in one Boston community said, "Dance!" They probably wouldn't have predicted what happened next: six older kids volunteered to learn Latin dance from professionals and become dance teachers!

The teens formed a group called *Ritmo en Acción* and began sharing the dance steps they learned. They taught classes at two elementary schools and one dance studio. The program grew quickly as more kids became teachers and more young children learned to dance. For many of the children, it was a way to learn more about Latin culture; for all the students, it was a chance to spend time with teen role models they admired.

Today, the program is a big success. Every year, over three hundred children sign up and participate in the classes where their instructors teach them salsa and other cultural dances—all free of charge! Both the instructors and their young students agree that dancing is a great way to have fun while staying out of trouble.

WANTED: Rock Stars and Role Models!

If you like music and being in the spotlight and you would like to have fun and make a difference in your community, then join the coolest, hippest, happiest kids in town—River City Rock Stars!

The River City Rock Stars are student performers who dance and sing to their favorite music. The group meets at the River City Community Center one evening a week. Each meeting starts with pizza and a demonstration by Troy Robbins, a.k.a. Hard Rock Robbins, a local legend who originated the group and is now its sponsor. He coaches Rock Star members in all aspects of performance. Each fall, Robbins creates a music video featuring that year's River City Rock Stars.

The best part of being a Rock Star is teaching young fans how to sing, dance, and have fun just like a Rock Star. Instead of being bored after school ends in the afternoon, Rock Stars teach songs and dance routines to struggling students in after-school workshops. The young students then take part in a Rock Star performance at their school.

Past Rock Star groups have done a phenomenal job of inspiring their young students. These letters from Rock Star fans say it all:

Dear Rock Stars,

It was awesome learning to sing and dance with you. You told me that I have to keep up my grades to stay in the group. I wasn't making good grades then. Now I am doing better in school because I want to join the Rock Stars someday. Thank you, Rock Stars!

Sincerely,
Gabriela

Dear Rock Stars,

You really do rock! I was very shy, but after working with you I found out that I love to dance. Performing on stage was incredible! It helped me make new friends. Now I'm teaching my friends all those cool moves.

Rock on,
Jesse

Would you like to help and inspire young students, too? Join us and take on a new and exciting role. Be someone young fans can admire. Be a Rock Star!

Rock Star Registration

Who: Sixth to eighth graders

Requirements: Good grades, teacher recommendations, parental permission

Where: River City Community Center

When: 7:00 P.M., Wednesday

43

Name _____ Date _____

Now answer Numbers 1 through 17 on your Answer Sheet. Base your answers on the article "Kids Making a Difference" and the flyer "WANTED: Rock Stars and Role Models!"

1 Read this sentence from the article.

> **All around the country, the power of older kids is making an impressive impact.**

What does the word *impressive* mean in the sentence above?

A. minor

B. ordinary

C. pleasing

D. remarkable

2 Which pair of words used in the article is most similar in meaning?

F. skills, pointers

G. impact, confidence

H. volunteered, formed

I. valuable, worthwhile

3 Read this sentence from the article.

> **The student tutors say they get a great experience from working with kids.**

Which syllable in the word *experience* has the schwa sound in the sentence above?

A. ex

B. pe

C. ri

D. ence

Name _____ Date _____

4 Read this sentence from the article.

> **Some kids learn to slam-dunk a basketball, while others learn the fundamentals of tennis.**

What does the word *fundamentals* mean in the sentence above?

F. basics

G. equipment

H. stories

I. tricks

5 How does the text structure of the section *Salsa Teachers in Boston* contribute to the development of the central idea in this section?

A. The author uses chronological order to show what happens during one *Ritmo en Acción* dance class.

B. The author uses description to show what types of dances the teens in *Ritmo en Acción* teach to young people.

C. The author uses cause-and-effect to show how *Ritmo en Acción* was formed and the effect it has on those involved.

D. The author uses comparison-contrast to show how *Ritmo en Acción* is unique among other dance programs in Boston.

6 Read this sentence from the article.

> **They probably wouldn't have predicted what happened next: six older kids volunteered to learn Latin dance from professionals and become dance teachers!**

What does the word *predicted* mean in the sentence above?

F. said what would happen in the future

G. doubted what could happen in the future

H. waited for what would happen in the future

I. demanded what should happen in the future

Name _____ Date _____

7 Read this sentence from the article.

> **For many of the children, it was a way to learn more about Latin culture.**

What is the final syllable of the word *culture* in the sentence above?

A. re

B. ure

C. ture

D. ulture

8 Read this sentence from the article.

> **Every year, over three hundred children sign up and participate in the classes, where their instructors teach them salsa and other cultural dances—all free of charge!**

What words help the reader understand what *participate* means in the sentence above?

F. *sign up*

G. *instructors*

H. *free of charge*

I. *cultural dances*

9 What is most likely the author's purpose for writing the flyer "WANTED: Rock Stars and Role Models!"?

A. to encourage older students to sign up for the River City Rock Stars group

B. to convince community members to attend the River City Rock Stars' performance

C. to explain to people about the impact that River City Rocks Stars has on young people

D. to entertain students with a story about a group of students who are making a difference

10 Which one of these words from the flyer has a negative connotation?

    F. bored

    G. fans

    H. routines

    I. sing

11 Which of the following best explains how the author supports the claim that the River City Rock Stars can make a difference?

    A. The author maintains a positive, encouraging tone throughout the flyer to draw readers in.

    B. The author includes two letters from kids who have participated in workshops to show how the Rock Stars have impacted them.

    C. The author includes the perspectives of several Rock Star members to show why they like being in the group and what it means to them.

    D. The author provides readers with registration requirements and details such as who can join the Rock Stars and where and when they meet.

12 Read this sentence from the flyer.

> **Past Rock Star groups have done a phenomenal job of inspiring their young students.**

What does the word *phenomenal* mean in the sentence above?

    F. difficult

    G. entertaining

    H. extraordinary

    I. thoughtful

13 Based on information in the flyer, students who are eligible to become River City Rock Stars must be

    A. struggling in school.

    B. earning good grades.

    C. trained musicians or dancers.

    D. recommended by Troy Robbins.

Name _____ Date _____

14 Read this sentence from the flyer.

>   **Performing on stage was incredible!**

Which word has the same suffix as the word *incredible* in the sentence above?

F. credit

G. dribble

H. reliable

I. sensible

15 One message that is the same in the article and the flyer is that volunteering helps kids

A. do their best.

B. make new friends.

C. become better athletes.

D. build career experience.

16 One difference between the article and the flyer is that

F. the article is a work of fiction and the flyer is a work of nonfiction.

G. the article was written to inform and the flyer was written to persuade.

H. the article shows kids in a positive light and the flyer focuses on kids' faults.

I. the article is mainly about Latin music and the flyer is mainly about rock-and-roll.

17 How are the Seattle tutoring program and River City Rock Stars program alike?

A. Both programs are led by local musicians.

B. Both programs involve playing games and making crafts.

C. In both programs, older students work with young struggling students.

D. In both programs, the younger students get to take part in a performance.

Read the passage "Winners" before answering Numbers 18 through 35.

Winners

A crowd of students stood talking and laughing in the school courtyard while they waited for the morning bell to ring. Suddenly a whistle pierced the quiet morning. When Gary looked toward the sound, he saw Laney in her morning patrol vest blocking the entrance and defying Javier to take another step. Javier was a new student from Mexico who had been enrolled in Gary's class the day before.

"Where do you think you're going?" she demanded.

Javier glanced around sheepishly, embarrassed to be the focus of everyone's attention. Gary immediately realized that Javier didn't understand what was happening and stepped forward before the situation could worsen.

"Javier is a new student," he told Laney, gesturing for Javier to come stand with him. Javier gratefully hurried away from the door and Laney's suspicious glare.

"I don't understand," Javier said with a bewildered look.

Gary explained that they had to wait for the bell before going into the building, but Javier still seemed confused.

Just then the bell rang and Gary pointed toward the door. "Now, we can go into the classroom," he said.

Javier observed the students moving toward the door and then grinned and nodded enthusiastically. "We can go in!" he said, pointing to the door.

As the rest of the students sat down and got out their materials for language arts, Mr. Parks explained to Javier that he should take his books and go to room 307 for his English lesson.

When Gary saw the confused expression on Javier's face, he wrote down the room number on a scrap of paper. Gary pointed at Javier and then at the door and then handed Javier the paper, telling him, "You need to go to room 307."

Javier stared at the number and then broke into a big smile. "I go here," he confirmed. "Thank you!"

Gary got a big kick out of the look that lit up Javier's face each time he figured out what someone meant. It was the same expression game show contestants get after giving the correct answer and winning a million dollars.

When it was time for geometry, Gary slumped in his chair and experienced his usual wave of dread. He was a competent student and did well in most subjects, but mathematics of any kind always made him feel like one big failure, and geometry in particular was like a foreign language.

Just as Mr. Parks wrote a page number on the board, Javier returned and eagerly got out his geometry book. Gary watched as Javier slowly turned the pages and studied the diagrams. He looked as engrossed as Gary did when he pored over the latest skateboard catalog!

Mr. Parks drew a right triangle on the board, labeled two sides with measurements, and wrote an x next to the third side. Then he turned to face the class, but before he could begin to explain the concept of using the two given measurements to find the missing one, Javier's hand shot up into the air.

Mr. Parks looked pleased, extending the chalk to Javier and asking, "Would you like to demonstrate how to find the value of x?"

Javier hurried to the board, quickly wrote the equation for finding x, and then solved it. Gary stared dumbfounded[1] at Javier's neat, confident calculations.

"Excellent work, Javier!" exclaimed Mr. Parks, clearly delighted and surprised. "If you keep improving your English, you may soon be up here doing *my* job!"

Javier returned to his seat, obviously happy to have shown his classmates that he was good at something, even if he didn't understand English well.

Gary leaned across the aisle and held up his open hand. Javier contemplated it for a minute and then seemed to recognize the gesture. As he gave Gary a high-five, he flashed his million-dollar winner's smile again.

Gary pointed to the geometry book in front of Javier and grimaced to show his exasperation. He shook his head and said, "*I do not understand.*"

Javier grinned and jerked his thumb to his chest. "I understand. I can help!"

Javier did help. He and Gary met during lunch to study. Each time Gary took a wrong turn in his calculations, Javier found ways to get him back on track. He drew pictures, made gestures, and pointed, and somehow Gary made sense of it all. After they got through a lesson, Javier held up his hand for another high-five. "Hit my head," he said.

"You mean *hand*," Gary said laughing. "Javier, my friend, you definitely need some help with your English!"

Javier laughed, too. "You can help?"

[1]**dumbfounded:** amazed or astonished

50

Gary considered the idea and said, "I'll be your English tutor if you keep those geometry lessons coming."

Javier happily agreed, and each afternoon, he helped Gary with his geometry homework. Gary, in turn, helped Javier with English.

When Mr. Parks returned the week's homework on Friday afternoon, Gary was hesitant to look at his grades, wondering if he'd misunderstood Javier's lessons. Reluctantly, he looked at his homework pages to see how he'd done.

"Javier, these are the highest math grades I've gotten in years!" Gary said. "Thanks to your help, of course," he quickly added.

"Yes, my friend," Javier said, nodding and holding up his hand for a high-five. "Hit my head!"

Javier grinned at his own joke, and then both boys burst out laughing.

"How about a skateboard lesson to thank you for tutoring me?" suggested Gary. "I'll teach you the English words for all the moves, too."

As the two headed to Gary's house to get skateboards, they were each wearing a million-dollar winner's smile.

Now answer Numbers 18 through 35 on your Answer Sheet. Base your answers on the passage "Winners."

18 Laney confronted Javier because he

    F. wouldn't speak English to her.

    G. tried to be the center of attention.

    H. tried to enter the class before the bell.

    I. blew a whistle in the school courtyard.

19 Read this sentence from the passage.

> **When Gary looked toward the sound, he saw Laney in her morning
> patrol vest blocking the entrance and defying Javier to take another
> step.**

What does the word *defying* mean in the sentence above?

A. challenging

B. helping

C. inviting

D. questioning

20 Which pair of words in the passage are most OPPOSITE in meaning?

F. dread, pored

G. eagerly, slowly

H. dumbfounded, surprised

I. obviously, enthusiastically

21 Read this sentence from the passage.

> **Gary immediately realized that Javier didn't understand what was
> happening and stepped forward before the situation could worsen.**

Which syllable in the word *happening* is often pronounced with the schwa sound
in the sentence above?

A. hap

B. pen

C. ni

D. ing

22 Read this sentence from the passage.

> **Gary immediately realized that Javier didn't understand what was
> happening and stepped forward before the situation could worsen.**

What is the final syllable of the word *worsen* in the sentence above?

   F. orsen

   G. rsen

   H. sen

   I. en

23 Read this sentence from the passage.

> **Gary got a big kick out of the look that lit up Javier's face each time he
> figured out what someone meant.**

What is the base word of the word *figured* in the sentence above?

   A. fig

   B. figur

   C. figure

   D. gure

24 What made Javier smile his "million-dollar winner's" smile?

   F. leaving the classroom

   G. understanding English

   H. studying his geometry book

   I. being the center of attention

25 Which word from the passage has a negative connotation?

   A. confirmed

   B. demanded

   C. explained

   D. suggested

26 Read this sentence from the passage.

> **When it was time for geometry, Gary slumped in his chair and
> experienced his usual wave of dread.**

Which word is a synonym for the word *slumped* as it is used in the
sentence above?

F. collapsed

G. slouched

H. stretched

I. turned

27 Read this sentence from the passage.

> **He was a competent student and did well in most subjects, but
> mathematics of any kind always made him feel like one big failure, and
> geometry in particular was like a foreign language.**

What words in the sentence above help the reader understand the meaning of the
word *competent*?

A. did well

B. most subjects

C. mathematics of any kind

D. big failure

28 Which of the following best describes how the author develops the passage's point
of view?

F. The author reveals both Javier and Gary's inner thoughts and feelings.

G. The author reveals Javier's inner thoughts and feelings, but readers must infer
Gary's thoughts and feelings.

H. The author reveals Gary's inner thoughts and feelings, but readers must infer
Javier's thoughts and feelings.

I. The author does not reveal any of the character's inner thoughts or feelings;
instead, readers must infer them.

29 Read this sentence from the passage.

> **Then he turned to face the class, but before he could begin to explain the concept of using the two given measurements to find the missing one, Javier's hand shot up into the air.**

What does the word *concept* mean in the sentence above?

A. idea

B. mystery

C. problem

D. secret

30 Read this sentence from the passage.

> **"Excellent work, Javier!" exclaimed Mr. Parks, clearly delighted and surprised.**

Which word has the same sounds as the underlined letters in *delighted* in the sentence above?

F. assign

G. digit

H. signature

I. weight

31 Why does Gary offer to tutor Javier in English?

A. Javier begs Gary to help him.

B. Mr. Parks asks Gary to help Javier.

C. Gary has lots of experience tutoring.

D. Javier first helps Gary with geometry.

Name _____ Date _____

32 Read this excerpt from the passage.

> **After they got through a lesson, Javier held up his hand for another high-five. "Hit my head," he said.**
>
> **"You mean *hand*," Gary said laughing. "Javier, my friend, you definitely need some help with your English!"**

Which of the following best describes the tone of the excerpt above?

F. childish

G. dramatic

H. playful

I. tense

33 Read this sentence from the passage.

> **Reluctantly, he looked at his homework pages to see how he'd done.**

What does the word *reluctantly* mean in the sentence above?

A. angrily

B. carefully

C. sadly

D. unwillingly

34 Which statement best describes the theme of this passage?

F. It is important to stand up for what you believe in.

G. Sometimes it can be difficult to make the right decision.

H. Everyone has strong suits, which they can use to help others.

I. Conflicts often stem from people misunderstanding each other.

Name _____ Date _____

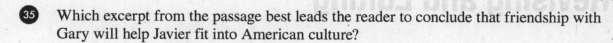

35 Which excerpt from the passage best leads the reader to conclude that friendship with Gary will help Javier fit into American culture?

A. "Gary watched as Javier slowly turned the pages and studied the diagrams. He looked as engrossed as Gary did when he pored over the latest skateboarding catalog!"

B. "Javier returned to his seat, obviously happy to have shown his classmates that he was good at something, even if he didn't understand English well."

C. "He and Gary met during lunch to study. Each time Gary took a wrong turn in his calculations, Javier found ways to get him back on track."

D. "'How about a skateboard lesson to thank you for tutoring me?' suggested Gary. 'I'll teach you the English words for all the moves, too.'"

Name _____ Date _____

Revising and Editing

Read the introduction and the passage "My Favorite Summer Place" before answering Numbers 1 through 7.

DeShaun wrote this passage about his favorite summer place. Read his passage and think about the changes he should make.

My Favorite Summer Place

(1) When the sweltering days of summer arrive, I love to go to Crystal Falls because everything about that place makes me feel happy, cool, and refreshed.

(2) The adventure begins at the trailhead which is located in Roosevelt Community Park. (3) From there, my family hike the two-mile long path that crisscrosses the pine-covered mountainside and climbs toward the falls. (4) The steep, rocky trail is definitely not for casual hikers! (5) We know we have reached the final stretch of the journey. (6) We hear the falls roaring and splashing. (7) The moment we hear the thunder of the falls, my sister Dorie and I are tempted to rush ahead. (8) Niether of us can wait to plunge into the icy water! (9) My mother warns my sister not to hurry and she warns me, too. (10) The rocks on the trail can be treacherous. (11) We continue to hike with our parents, but the anticipation is hard to contain!

(12) Finally, we reach the place where the giant waterfall pours over a tall, rocky cliff. (13) The cool mist from the waterfall feels delightful, so I pull off my shoes and eagerly wade into the shallow pool.

(14) After cooling off, I walk around to the pool ledge behind the curtain of falling water. (15) Dorie looks blurry as she waves to me from the other side. (16) I shout loudly to her. (17) She can't hear my words. (18) The roar of the falls is deafening.

(19) I hope you have the opportunity to visit Crystal Falls sometime. (20) It's a demanding hike up to the falls. (21) I guarantee you that it's worth the effort. (22) Once you experience it for yourself, I'm certain you'll agree that Crystal Falls is a summer paradise!

Now answer Numbers 1 through 7 on your Answer Sheet. Base your answers on the changes DeShaun should make.

1 Which sentence could best be added before sentence 2?

   A. Swimming at the falls is a real treat.

   B. Crystal Falls is a tall, noisy waterfall.

   C. My sister Dorie can't hike as fast as I can.

   D. The hike to Crystal Falls is part of the fun.

2 What change should be made in sentence 3?

   F. change *there* to **their**

   G. change *hike* to **hikes**

   H. change *climbs* to **climb**

   I. change the period to a question mark

Name _____ Date _____

3 What is the best way to combine sentences 5 and 6?

A. We know we have reached the final stretch of the journey but we hear the falls roaring and splashing.

B. We know we have reached the final stretch of the journey when we hear the falls roaring and splashing.

C. We know we have reached the final stretch of the journey unless we hear the falls roaring and splashing.

D. We know we have reached the final stretch of the journey although we hear the falls roaring and splashing.

4 What change should be made in sentence 8?

F. change *Niether* to **Neither**

G. change *us* to **we**

H. change *plunge* to **plunged**

I. change the exclamation point to a period

5 What is the best way to combine sentences 9 and 10?

A. My mother warns me to not hurry and my sister, too, since the rocks can be treacherous.

B. My mother warns my sister and I not to hurry, but the rocks on the trail can be treacherous.

C. My mother warns my sister and I not to hurry and the rocks on the trail can be treacherous, too.

D. My mother warns my sister and me not to hurry because the rocks on the trail can be treacherous.

6   What is the best way to combine sentences 16, 17, and 18?

    F.   After I shout loudly to her, she can't hear my words so the roar of the falls is deafening.

    G.   I shout loudly to her, and she can't hear my words but the roar of the falls is deafening.

    H.   Since I shout loudly to her, she can't hear my words so the roar of the falls is deafening.

    I.   Although I shout loudly to her, she can't hear my words because the roar of the falls is deafening.

7   What is the best way to combine sentences 20 and 21?

    A.   It's a demanding hike up to the falls, I guarantee you that it's worth the effort.

    B.   It's a demanding hike up to the falls, or I guarantee you that it's worth the effort.

    C.   It's a demanding hike up to the falls, but I guarantee you that it's worth the effort.

    D.   It's a demanding hike up to the falls and I guarantee you that it's worth the effort.

Read the introduction and the passage "Our Crazy Canoe Trip" before answering Numbers 8 through 14.

Eva wrote this passage about a canoe trip with her family. Read her passage and think about the changes she should make.

Our Crazy Canoe Trip

(1) Last summer my family went on a memorable canoe trip.

(2) We expected a relaxed float down the river. (3) It turned out to be a wild ride!

(4) Dad and I paddled one canoe, and Mom paddled another with my little brother, Charlie. (5) Things started out nice and easy. (6) It wasn't long before things changed.

(7) In one narrow part of the river, trees extended out over the water. (8) As Charlie battled anacondas that he imagined were hanging from the branches, he made one serious errur. (9) He swatted at them with his paddle.

(10) Suddenly, we heard a deafening buzz, and we realized that Charlie had disturbed a beehive! (11) Mom yelled, "Everyone into the water!"

(12) Minutes later, the bees had departed but we were in a mess.

(13) Both canoes were overturned, and our supplies floating around us.

(14) Thankfully, our life jackets kept us afloat while we loaded the canoes and started down the river again.

(15) Our next mishap occurred at the rapids. (16) I love zipping over rushing water, but this time the water was *too* fast. (17) It spun our canoe sideways and shoved us up onto a large rock. (18) Swirling below us, our

paddles couldn't even reach the water! (19) Thinking quickly, Dad got out and pushed the canoe free. (20) He barely made it back into our canoe before it rushed downstream!

(21) Back in calm water, Charlie dipped his sunglasses in the river to rinse them. (22) The sparkle of the metal frames attracted some fish and one jumped into the air. (23) Plop! (24) It landed right in Charlie's lap. (25) The fish gave such a start that Charlie jumped up, causing the boat to tip. (26) Charlie, Mom, and the fish all ended up in the river.

(27) We repacked their canoe we all agreed that our next trip would be a bike ride!

Now answer Numbers 8 through 14 on your Answer Sheet. Base your answers on the changes Eva should make.

8 What is the best way to combine sentences 2 and 3?

F. We expected a relaxed float down the river, or it turned out to be a wild ride!

G. So we expected a relaxed float down the river it turned out to be a wild ride!

H. We expected a relaxed float down the river since it turned out to be a wild ride!

I. Although we expected a relaxed float down the river, it turned out to be a wild ride!

9 What is the best way to combine sentences 5 and 6?

A. Things started out nice and easy, it wasn't long before things changed.

B. Things started out nice and easy, or it wasn't long before things changed.

C. Things started out nice and easy, but it wasn't long before things changed.

D. Since things started out nice and easy, it wasn't long before things changed.

Name _____ Date _____

10 What change should be made in sentence 8?

    F. insert a comma after *Charlie*

    G. change *battled* to **battles**

    H. change *errur* to **error**

    I. delete the comma after *branches*

11 What change should be made in sentence 13?

    A. change *canoes* to **canoe**

    B. change *and* to **but**

    C. insert **were** before *floating*

    D. change *us* to **we**

12 What is the best way to revise sentence 18?

    F. Swirling, our paddles couldn't even reach below the water!

    G. Our paddles couldn't even reach the water swirling below us!

    H. Swirling below our paddles, we couldn't even reach the water!

    I. Our paddles, swirling below us, couldn't even reach the water!

13 What change should be made in sentence 25?

    A. insert **him** after *gave*

    B. insert a comma after *start*

    C. change *jumped* to **jumps**

    D. change *the boat* to **it**

14 What is the best way to revise sentence 27?

    F. We repacked their canoe, we all agreed that our next trip would be a bike ride!

    G. As we repacked their canoe, we all agreed that our next trip would be a bike ride!

    H. We repacked their canoe, or we all agreed that our next trip would be a bike ride!

    I. Until we repacked their canoe, we all agreed that our next trip would be a bike ride!

Read the introduction and the article "Water Pollution" before answering Numbers 15 through 20.

Molly wrote this article about water pollution. Read her article and think about the changes she should make.

Water Pollution

(1) However, it is still a big problem. (2) That is why it be important for everyone to try and do their part to help. (3) Doing everyday things the right way can help prevent water pollution.

(4) Each weekend, many people spend working in their yards.

(5) Some people might use chemicals to kill weeds and pests. (6) They might also spread fertilizer to help plants and flowers grow. (7) These chemicals can soak into the ground and pollute underground water sources. (8) It is important to read the labels, to help limit the impact of these things on the water supply, on these products. (9) The chemicals should be used in moderation and only as directed. (10) People can also seek out natural alternatives to chemicals for pest control or fertilizer.

(11) People can also cause water pollution if they wash their cars nor change the oil in their cars. (14) Soap and oily dirt from car washing can flow into the street and then into storm drains. (15) It is important to only use soaps that are not harmful to the environment when washing a car.

(16) Instead of taking their cars to a mechanic for an oil change, some people change the oil themselves. (17) When doing this, it is important that the old oil is taken to a place that accepts old oil for proper disposal.

(18) It is expensive to make polluted water useble again.

(19) Preventing pollution in the first place makes good sense. (20) People can make a difference if they follow a few simple rules.

Now answer Numbers 15 through 20 on your Answer Sheet. Base your answers on the changes Molly should make.

15 Which sentence could best be added before sentence 1?

   A. Some towns depend on water for fishing or recreation.

   B. Many laws have been passed to prevent water pollution.

   C. Cars can cause water pollution in several different ways.

   D. All humans need water to survive, especially when it is hot outside.

16 What change should be made in sentence 2?

   F. change *be* to **is**

   G. change *try* to **tried**

   H. change *and* to **or**

   I. insert a comma after *part*

17 What change should be made in sentence 4?

    A. delete the comma after *weekend*

    B. change *many* to **lots and lots of**

    C. insert **time** after *spend*

    D. change *their* to **there**

18 What is the best way to revise sentence 8?

    F. It is important to read, to help limit the impact of these things on the water supply, the labels on these products.

    G. To help limit the impact of these things on the water supply, it is important to read the labels on these products.

    H. On the water supply, it is important to read the labels on these products, to help limit the impact of these things.

    I. To help limit the impact of these things on these products, it is important to read the labels on the water supply.

19 What change should be made in sentence 11?

    A. change *cause* to **causes**

    B. change *if* to **although**

    C. change *nor* to **or**

    D. change *their* to **your**

20 What change should be made in sentence 18?

    F. change *is* to **are**

    G. change *make* to **made**

    H. delete *water* after **polluted**

    I. change *useble* to **usable**

Name _____ Date _____

Writing Arguments

Read the article "Education in Japan" before responding to the prompt.

Education in Japan

Can you imagine attending school on Saturdays instead of having time off to relax? Many Japanese families pay so that students can do just that! Succeeding in school is extremely important in Japanese culture. That is why parents pay for their children to attend extra classes called *juku* in the evenings and on weekends.

Like American students, Japanese students attend elementary school for six years and junior high school for three years. Those nine years of education are mandatory[1] for all students. However, the three years of high school offered to Japanese students are optional. Students must pass a difficult test and pay tuition if they want to go beyond junior high school. In spite of these obstacles, most students meet the high standards and pay the fees so they can graduate from high school. Very few ever drop out.

At the beginning of the school day, Japanese students perform a morning ritual of bowing and giving their teacher a respectful greeting. Many wear school uniforms, which they are expected to keep neat and clean at all times.

The school curriculum in Japan is challenging and generally includes memorizing a great deal of information. Elementary and junior high school students usually work as a class rather than individually or in small groups as American students often do. The Japanese students sometimes recite their lessons aloud and in unison. The classroom teacher may also teach students to play musical instruments.

At lunch, the students usually go to the cafeteria and prepare their own food. While in the kitchen, they wear masks to avoid contaminating food and spreading germs. They return to their classroom to eat and then clean up after the meal. As in America, recess is spent playing active games, such as soccer.

Once afternoon classes are over, students in most schools are expected to clean their classroom and school. They scrub, sweep, and mop until everything is sparkling clean. Then, as they leave their classroom, they bow to their teachers and thank them.

[1]**mandatory:** required

Name _____ Date _____

After dismissal from class, most students remain at school for several more hours to attend clubs or extra classes. They learn computer skills, English, sports, card games, homemaking skills, and music. Many students also attend *juku* for tutoring to help them keep up with their most difficult subjects of study. Others go to *juku* courses that prepare them for the challenging high school entrance exams.

The diligent work that Japanese students do clearly shows in test score results. In exams that compare student achievement in countries around the world, Japanese students always rank at or near the top.

Name _____ Date _____

Now respond to the prompt. Base your response on the article "Education in Japan."

> According to the article "Education in Japan," succeeding in school is very important in Japanese culture.
>
> Think about whether or not American schools should be more like Japanese schools.
>
> Write a response that explains why or why not, using details from the article and your own school experiences to support your response.

Planning Page

Use this space to make your notes before you begin writing. The writing on this page will NOT be scored.

_____

_____

_____

_____

_____

_____

_____

_____

_____

_____

_____

_____

_____

**Begin writing your response here. The writing on this page and the next page
WILL be scored.**

_____

_____

_____

_____

_____

_____

_____

_____

_____

_____

_____

_____

_____

_____

_____

_____

_____

_____

_____

_____

_____

_____

_____

_____

_____

_____

_____

_____

_____

_____

_____

_____

_____

_____

_____

_____

_____

_____

_____

_____

_____

_____

_____

_____

_____

_____

_____

_____

_____

Name _____ Date _____

Reading Complex Text

Read the journal "Our Compost Journal" and the article "Backyard Composting: It's Only Natural." As you read, stop and answer each question. Use evidence from the journal and the article to support your answers.

Our Compost Journal

Sunday, April 28th

My dad read in the newspaper recently that Americans generate approximately 240 million tons of garbage each year. A huge portion of the garbage that winds up in dumps and landfills consists of food waste and yard trimmings! After hearing that, I peered into our family's kitchen trash can; sure enough, it contained lots of food waste. Our family has decided to embark on a household project to cut back on household waste: we are going to turn our food and yard waste into compost for our garden. I am in charge of keeping a journal of our composting project.

Before we started, I wanted to do some research to learn more about compost. In a book I checked out from the library, I learned that compost, also called humus, is organic, decomposed material that can be used as a natural fertilizer in the garden. When you make compost, you mimic the natural process of decomposition that takes place on forest floors. Over time, fallen leaves and other dead plants and animals begin to decay, or break down. Tiny microorganisms help the plant and animal matter break down into rich, dark, and earthy humus. My mom, our family's garden expert, says that humus is packed with nutrients that provide the food needed to help plants grow. The flowers and vegetables in our garden will love it, she says!

---

1 What does the word *decomposition* mean as used in the section above?

_____

_____

_____

Name _____ Date _____

Saturday, May 4th

Today, we built a bin for our compost pile. We thought about just creating a large pile in a corner of our backyard, but we decided that a simple bin would help contain the compost. One of our neighbors gave us four wooden pallets. While I held them steady, my brother Caleb nailed the pallets together to form a large box. Then, we helped Dad secure the box by driving four stakes into the ground, one at each corner of the box, and used rope to bind the box to the stakes. When we were finished, we stepped back to admire our work. Now it's time for the real dirty work to begin!

Sunday, May 5th

We are beginning to save our food waste for the compost pile. My brother is in charge of finding out what we can and cannot compost. According to him, everything we toss into our compost bin must be organic. That means it must be derived from once-living organisms. Our compost must also be a combination of "green" and "brown" materials. Caleb posted a list on the refrigerator that explains both materials. "Green" materials are rich in the nutrient nitrogen. Grass clippings, weeds, fruit, vegetable scraps, coffee grounds, eggshells, and tea bags are examples of green materials. "Brown" materials are carbon-rich. They include: wood chips, pine needles, straw, sawdust, fireplace ashes, hair, fur, paper, cardboard, and newspaper—all cut into small pieces. Caleb also made a list of things that we CANNOT compost: meat, fish, dairy products, eggs, and oily and fatty foods. These foods are difficult to break down; plus, they emit bad odors and would attract lots of pests to our compost pile!

Sunday, May 26th

It has been a few weeks since I have updated the compost journal. I thought for sure we'd have humus by now, but I guess it can take several months for the materials in our pile to break down. My dad says we can help the process along by adding some soil to the pile, keeping the pile damp (but not too wet), and occasionally turning the materials with a pitchfork. Turning the pile helps circulate oxygen, which, in addition to air and water, is a key ingredient for decomposition.

Thursday, June 7th

Early this morning, I noticed that steam was rising from our compost bin. Mom explained that as material in our bin rots, heat and carbon dioxide are produced. This is why we see steam. The steam is a good sign! It means that the decay process is well underway. The heat is killing harmful pests, diseases, and the seeds of weeds. I found this diagram to show what's going on in our compost bin.

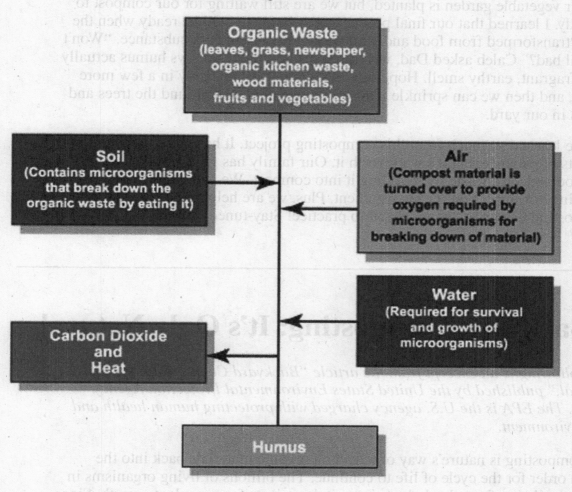

How Compost is Made

Organic Waste
(leaves, grass, newspaper, organic kitchen waste, wood materials, fruits and vegetables)

Soil
(Contains microorganisms that break down the organic waste by eating it)

Air
(Compost material is turned over to provide oxygen required by microorganisms for breaking down of material)

Water
(Required for survival and growth of microorganisms)

Carbon Dioxide and Heat

Humus

❷ Use the diagram and the section before it to explain what is needed to make compost and what is produced in the process.

_____

_____

_____

Sunday, June 17th

Our vegetable garden is planted, but we are still waiting for our compost to be ready. I learned that our final product—our humus—will be ready when the pile is transformed from food and yard waste into a rich, dark substance. "Won't it smell bad?" Caleb asked Dad, wrinkling his nose up. Dad says humus actually has a fragrant, earthy smell. Hopefully the humus will be ready in a few more weeks, and then we can sprinkle it all over our garden and around the trees and shrubs in our yard.

I've learned so much from this composting project. It has taken some effort and lots of patience, but it's well worth it. Our family has greatly reduced our food and yard waste by recycling it into compost. We feel good about lessening our impact on the environment. Plus, we are helping our garden grow! Composting is a great "green" habit to practice! Stay-tuned, journal…

Backyard Composting: It's Only Natural

The following is an excerpt from the article "Backyard Composting: It's Only Natural," published by the United States Environmental Protection Agency (EPA). The EPA is the U.S. agency charged with protecting human health and the environment.

Composting is nature's way of recycling organic materials back into the soil in order for the cycle of life to continue. The billions of living organisms in healthy soil transform dead plants into vital nutrients for new plant growth. Since healthy plants come from healthy soil, one of the best ways you can build healthy soil in your garden and lawn is by using compost. You can easily make compost with landscape trimmings and food scraps in your own backyard. With a small investment in time, you can improve the health and appearance of your yard, save money on fertilizers and mulch, all while preserving natural resources and protecting the health of your family and pets.

3 Describe how the author promotes composting in the section above.

_____

_____

_____

Why compost?

- **It's earth-friendly:** Food scraps and yard waste make up 20-30% of the waste stream. Making compost keeps these materials out of landfills, where they take up precious space and release methane, a greenhouse gas 21 times more potent than carbon dioxide emissions in the atmosphere.

- **It benefits your yard:** Compost improves soil structure and texture, increases the soil's ability to hold both water and air, improves soil fertility, and stimulates healthy root development in plants.

- **It's easy:** You can start with just leaves and grass, then work your way towards composting your food scraps.

- **It saves money:** Adding compost to your garden can reduce or eliminate the need to buy chemical fertilizers or compost. If you pay for the amount of trash hauled, composting can also cut down on your trash costs.

4 Compare and contrast how the authors of "Our Compost Journal" and "Backyard Composting: It's Only Natural" present information about composting.

_____

_____

_____

_____

_____

Name _____ Date _____

Reading and Analyzing Text

Read the passage "Not What I Thought" before answering Numbers 1 through 6.

Not What I Thought

Even as a little child, Emma hated spaghetti because she thought it was slimy. She couldn't handle tapioca pudding or cottage cheese either. When Emma heard that her class was going to make pasta from scratch, she groaned piteously[1].

"Pasta is disgusting—it reminds me of worms," Emma complained secretly to Jonah. They both chuckled, stopping only when Mrs. Buckingham glanced sternly in their direction.

Friday morning, the entire class gathered in the cafeteria kitchen and split into work groups. Each group was to make tomato sauce, pasta, or antipasto[2] salad. Just as Emma had feared, she was assigned to the "pasta" group, along with her friends Jonah and Arturo.

After the three washed their hands, Jonah measured three pounds of flour and poured it into a bowl. Arturo carved a crater in the hill of flour, and then Jonah cracked a dozen eggs into it. Meanwhile, Emma stood by herself with her arms crossed, wishing her stomach would stop somersaulting at the sight of all those slimy eggs. Since Mrs. Buckingham had given each of the groups a detailed set of instructions, everyone knew exactly what to do. The next step would be to mix the dough by hand.

"Each group has to be certain that everyone participates," Mrs. Buckingham called out to the entire class, and of course, Arturo and Jonah stared directly at Emma.

"This step is all yours," Jonah announced unsympathetically with a mischievous grimace.

[1] **piteously:** in a pathetic way

[2] **antipasto:** a course of appetizers consisting of an assortment of foods

"You'd really rather do the kneading, wouldn't you?" Emma pleaded, looking sideways at Arturo.

"Nope, not me," Arturo replied, grinning and obviously hoping for a little extra drama.

Giving up hope, Emma grimaced as she pushed up her right sleeve and gripped the mixing bowl. She closed her eyes as she inserted her free hand directly into the eggs. Making a face at the sloshing sound they made as she turned the bowl, she squished them into the flour with her fingers. She did it again, faster and faster, and suddenly she realized that she enjoyed the rhythm and the feel of the dough. It was soft like skin yet sticky like gum. As she continued to spin the bowl and mix them, the flour and eggs became one perfect pillow of dough.

Mrs. Buckingham smiled approvingly at Emma. "Remember, Emma, as soon as the dough is an even consistency, knead it for twelve more minutes. Those twelve minutes are the secret to good pasta."

"Okay, you're off the hook. Give us a turn, too," Arturo teased, but he could tell she wasn't going to give up her share of the group's work. After twelve minutes, Jonah covered the dough with a towel, and the three of them cleaned up their work table. After the dough had risen, Mrs. Buckingham set up the pasta making machine. Arturo and Jonah took turns putting dough into the top of the machine and rotating the handle, while Emma caught the strands of fresh linguini in a clean bowl.

By 11:00 A.M., the class meal was almost ready: sauce simmered on the stove, bread toasted in the oven, and antipasto platters waited in the refrigerators. At 11:30 A.M., a huge pot of water started boiling to cook the pasta, and three minutes later, Emma's group drained the linguini and put it into big bowls, enough for everyone.

"Well, what do you think?" Mrs. Buckingham asked Emma, who was slurping a noodle into her mouth.

Emma answered her teacher with a big "thumbs up." After she finished chewing and wiping some of the sauce from her chin, she admitted, "It's absolutely delicious—not what I thought at all."

Name _____ Date _____

Now answer Numbers 1 through 6 on your Answer Sheet. Base your answers on the passage "Not What I Thought."

1 The children are preparing the spaghetti lunch for

    A. all of their classmates.

    B. everyone in the school.

    C. the principal and teachers.

    D. their teachers and parents.

2 What quality does Emma possess that is important to the passage's plot?

    F. She has a big appetite.

    G. She is disgusted by slimy things.

    H. She is curious about anything new.

    I. She gets along well with classmates.

3 Why do Jonah and Arturo leave Emma to knead the pasta dough?

    A. They want to watch her squirm.

    B. They already have experience kneading dough.

    C. They want to make her do the most difficult task.

    D. The dough's consistency makes them uncomfortable.

4 Read this sentence from the passage.

> **"Okay, you're off the hook. Give us a turn, too," Arturo teased, but he
> could tell she wasn't going to give up her share of the group's work.**

What does the phrase *off the hook* mean in the sentence above?

    F. free from a responsibility

    G. unwilling to perform a duty

    H. thoroughly enjoying something

    I. no longer allowed to do something

Name _____ Date _____

5 Read this sentence from the passage.

> After she finished chewing and wiping some of the sauce from her chin, she admitted, "It's absolutely delicious—not what I thought at all."

What does the word *admitted* mean in the sentence above?

A. acknowledged

B. argued

C. challenged

D. exclaimed

6 Which of the following best expresses the theme of this passage?

F. Persistence will lead to success.

G. Trying new things can be rewarding.

H. You have to believe in yourself to achieve your goal.

I. Give people a second chance—they might surprise you.

Read the article "Do You Want to Write a Poem?" before answering Numbers 7 through 12.

Winter's End
by Pamela Love

Late February
Icicles drip days away
Splashing into spring

Do You Want to Write a Poem?

by Myra Cohn Livingston
illustarted by Julie Kim

The word "haiku" means "a beginning phrase." A haiku was originally the beginning of a longer poem; the first 17 syllables were written to introduce the reader to the rest of the poem. Today haiku is considered a poetic form in itself.

Some of you might know that the short poem at the top of this page is called a *haiku*. Haiku poetry has been written in Japan for hundreds of years and has become popular in the United States. There are specific rules for writing haiku, but all most people know is that the poem is made up of 17 syllables, that it is usually written in three lines, and that it does not use rhyme.

The first rule for writing a haiku is that the poem must always refer to something in nature or use what is called a "season word." Many of the haiku you read refer to nature symbols of Japan, but unless you have visited Japan, you will be better off writing about things you know in your own country. For instance, if you read about a cherry blossom in a Japanese haiku, it means spring. Different flowers are more familiar signs of spring in other places, so you might want to write about snowdrops, crocuses, or daffodils if they grow near you. You do not have to use the words "spring," "summer," "autumn," or "winter" to name the season when you write a haiku—the word "snow," for example, becomes a season word for "winter."

Another rule is that the haiku must be about *one* thing only. A haiku is not a poem that describes several different subjects or events. A good writer of haiku looks at one thing carefully and writes about only that.

The third rule is that a haiku must be written as though you are just seeing or experiencing what you write about. It should happen *now*, not yesterday or the day before or last year. Therefore, haiku is usually written in the present tense.

The next rule is that a good haiku must present a clear picture of something you want to think about further. It paints a picture in words that stirs your imagination and makes you eager to find out more.

Remember, too, that when you have only 17 syllables, it is important to choose your words carefully and not repeat any.

A good way to get haiku ideas is to look outside or take a walk. Maybe you'll see a snail as the poet Issa did:

Well! Hello down there friend snail!
When did you arrive in such a hurry?

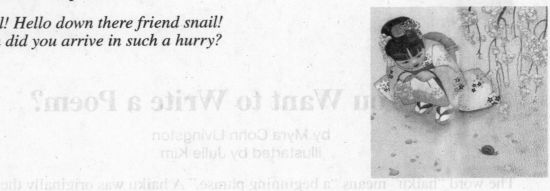

Or you might want to warn the butterflies, as the poet Shosen did:

> *Butterflies, beware!*
> *Needles of pines can be sharp*
> *in a gusty wind!*

If you are just beginning to write haiku, you might find it easier to write as though you were talking to whatever subject you choose—a butterfly, cricket, fly, or snail; or even the moon, stars, sun, wind, or rain.

Now it's your turn to write a haiku! Choose your words carefully, draw a vivid picture with them, and let your imagination run wild. . . .

Now answer Numbers 7 through 12 on your Answer Sheet. Base your answers on the article "Do You Want to Write a Poem?"

7 The poem "Winter's End" compares the

　　A. end of fall and growing icicles.

　　B. coming of winter and soft rain.

　　C. end of spring and violent storms.

　　D. coming of spring and melting icicles.

8 Read this sentence from the article.

> **Many of the haiku you read refer to nature symbols of Japan, but unless you have visited Japan, you will be better off writing about things you know in your own country.**

What does the word *symbols* mean in the sentence above?

　　F. essential characteristics

　　G. environments or natural habitats

　　H. things that represents other things

　　I. different components that make up a whole

9 The author's main purpose in writing this article is

　　A. to explain to readers how to write a haiku poem.

　　B. to entertain readers with a series of haiku poems.

　　C. to convince readers that a haiku is the highest form of poetry.

　　D. to explain the difference between haiku poetry in Japan and the United States.

10 Which pair of words from the article are most similar in meaning?

　　F. clear, vivid

　　G. introduce, refer

　　H. specific, familiar

　　I. originally, carefully

Name _____ Date _____

11 Read this sentence from the article.

> **It paints a picture in words that stirs your imagination and makes you eager to find out more.**

What does the word *imagination* mean as used in the sentence above?

A. the act of undergoing change

B. the act of making up one's mind

C. the process of forming new ideas

D. the state of experiencing strong feelings

12 The haiku examples from the poets Issa and Shosen support the author's claim that haiku writers

F. must choose precisely and carefully and not repeat any words.

G. might be inspired by looking outside or going for a walk outdoors.

H. must not write as if they are talking directly to their subject.

I. must use "season words," such as *summer* or *spring*.

Read the article "Alaska's Long, Cold Race" before answering Numbers 13 through 17.

Alaska's Long, Cold Race

Alaska's Iditarod Trail Sled Dog Race, held once every year in March, is the longest dogsled race in the world. During the Iditarod, dog teams and their human leaders, called mushers, cover over 1,150 miles in ten to seventeen days.

History

Beginning in the 1880s, with the discovery of gold, prospectors[1] flocked to Alaska to seek their fortune. Arriving on the coast, they followed trails to the interior, using dog-drawn sleds to travel hundreds of miles of frozen wilderness. Their main route from Anchorage to Nome is known today as the Iditarod Trail.

In the 1920s, airplanes began to replace dogsleds as a means of getting around the Alaskan wilderness. In the early 1960s, the snowmobile (the "iron dog") was invented, and dogsled teams fell into disuse. However, the one-hundredth anniversary of Alaska's statehood was approaching. Increased interest in Alaska's spirit and history led to the idea for a dogsled race.

A local historian named Dorothy Page, one of the planners for the 1967 centennial[2], had the idea. She suggested the Iditarod Trail as the route, and musher groups backed her enthusiastically. Volunteers, who have played a big part in the race from the beginning, began to clear brush from the long disused trail.

In 1967 the first Iditarod was run as part of Alaska's Centennial. That initial race was only 27 miles long. By 1973, the Trail had been restored all the way to Nome, and twenty-two mushers raced over its 1,150-mile length. The race has been held every year since then.

Route

The race begins in Anchorage (see map), and the teams wind through many towns, or checkpoints, such as Rainy Pass and Safety, before crossing the finish line in Nome. In even-numbered years, the race follows a northern route. In odd-numbered years, it follows a southern route that includes the old mining town of Iditarod. This change of route allows time for smaller towns to recover from the impact of the race.

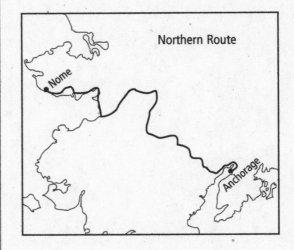

Northern Route

Nome

Anchorage

---

[1] **prospectors:** people who explore an area for mineral deposits such as gold

[2] **centennial:** a hundredth anniversary

88

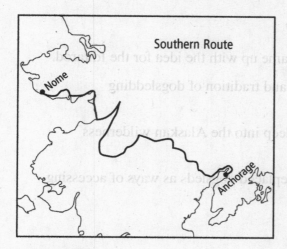

Southern Route

Nome

Anchorage

Competitors

According to the official Web site of the Iditarod, the competitors come from all walks of life and all over the world: "Fishermen, lawyers, doctors, miners, artists, natives, Canadians, Swiss, French, and others." About fifty to seventy mushers finish the grueling race each year.

Some of the mushers have made Iditarod history. For example, Rick Swenson is a five-time winner. He's also entered twenty Iditarod races and never finished out of the top ten. In 1978, Dick Mackey won the race from Swenson by

only one second. Four-time winner Susan Butcher was the first woman to place in the top ten. Libby Riddles was the first woman to win the race, in 1985.

Of course the teams are really contending with nature. March in Alaska can be brutal. The trail runs through wild mountains and dense forests and across rivers whose winter ice may be melting. Temperatures can be far below freezing, especially at night. Blizzards, sleet, and biting wind add to the hazards.

Popularity

The Iditarod attracts competitors because it is the longest, most challenging race of its kind in the world. Only the best teams can vie for the prize, and those that finish have reason to be proud. Perhaps one reason the Iditarod is so popular with spectators is that it gives them a chance to enjoy Alaska's breathtaking natural beauty. In any case, every spring, the crowds that line the trail to cheer on the mushers are reminded of the state's spirit and its history, just as Dorothy Page hoped.

Now answer Numbers 13 through 17 on your Answer Sheet. Base your answers on the article "Alaska's Long, Cold Race."

13 Read this sentence from the article.

> **Volunteers, who have played a big part in the race from the beginning, began to clear brush from the long disused trail.**

Which word is a synonym for the word *disused*, as it is used in the sentence above?

A. abandoned

B. ancient

C. famous

D. historic

Name _____ Date _____

14 What is the main idea of the section *History*?

   F. A local historian named Dorothy Page came up with the idea for the Iditarod.

   G. The Iditarod commemorates the history and tradition of dogsledding in Alaska.

   H. During the 1880s, prospectors traveled deep into the Alaskan wilderness seeking gold.

   I. Airplanes and snowmobiles eventually replaced dogsleds as ways of accessing the Alaskan wilderness.

15 Which detail in the text do the maps best help to clarify?

   A. The Iditarod begins in Anchorage, Alaska, and ends in Nome, Alaska.

   B. Since 1967, the race has extended from 27 miles to 1,150 miles in length.

   C. Depending on the year, the Iditarod follows either a northern or southern route.

   D. Competitors in the Iditarod cross mountains, forests, and icy rivers over the course of the race.

16 An idea of the difficulty of the race is given by facts about

   F. transportation in Alaska.

   G. the popularity of the race.

   H. mushers who run the race.

   I. the land and the weather conditions.

17 Which of the following excerpts from the article best conveys the author's viewpoint on the Iditarod?

   A. "Alaska's Iditarod Trail Sled Dog Race, held once every year in March, is the longest dogsled race in the world."

   B. "She suggested the Iditarod Trail as the route, and musher groups backed her enthusiastically."

   C. "According to the official Web site of the Iditarod, the competitors come from all walks of life and all over the world. . . ."

   D. "The Iditarod attracts competitors because it is the longest, most challenging race of its kind in the world."

Read the passage "Beginner's Mind" before answering Numbers 18 through 22.

Beginner's Mind

Back in the spring, when she chose to go to Tae Kwon Do camp, Felicia was really excited about her summer. However, now that she's here, she feels differently. She's been interested in martial arts for many years but never practiced before. Many of the campers she has met since arriving here this morning have been coming to this camp for several years. She's sure she will be the only one with a beginner's belt. She looks at herself in the bathroom mirror, smooths her new white uniform, and wonders how she looks.

Nevertheless, Felicia joins a group of laughing girls on their way to the practice hall. They introduce themselves, retelling the joke that had amused them, and Felicia laughs with the group. At the entrance to the practice room, Jill, a third-year camper, introduces herself as Felicia's partner. Adjusting Felicia's uniform, she explains how partnering works: "You'll take the place immediately behind me, and follow what I do. I'm sure you'll do great."

Removing their shoes, the campers enter the big, bright space and silently line up in straight columns, each separated by a comfortable distance. The practice room seems calm and inviting, and even though the windows are shaded, the shapes of the mountains surrounding the camp are visible. The wooden floor feels solid under Felicia's feet as she lines up behind Jill, thankfully, in the very back row.

Annie, Felicia's counselor and today's instructor, steps to the front of the room, places her palms together in front of her chest, and bows from the waist. Everyone else returns the gesture.

"Welcome," says Annie. "We have a few beginners with us, so let's begin with the rules; we'll recite these at each session." Felicia is familiar with these, since they were printed on the materials she received with her uniform.

As she echoes them with the campers, she glances around secretly to see several other girls with beginner's belts in the back row. "I'm not the only beginner," she thinks, relieved.

"We will begin today with a stretching demonstration. Stretching is one of the most important parts of practice, and this series of stretches will begin each practice session." Annie demonstrates a series of stretches, and the campers do the stretches with her. Then the campers do the series by themselves while

Annie walks around, correcting their positions as necessary. The stretches are complicated, so Felicia keeps her eyes glued on Jill. At one point she's almost touching the floor with one leg crook-kneed in front of her and the other leg stretched straight out behind, but she's concentrating too hard on doing the stretch correctly to worry about what she looks like.

The stretching continues, and Felicia starts to feel more comfortable. She likes the fact that all the campers are doing the same thing; she doesn't feel out of place, just part of the group.

After a while, Annie dismisses the class with a bow, and Felicia is surprised to find it is lunchtime. She follows the campers as they silently exit the practice room. Outside, Jill approaches Felicia and says, "See, you're a natural. I told you you'd do great." Felicia smiles and thanks Jill for being her partner. No longer worried about the summer ahead, Felicia grins widely and can't wait until the afternoon practice session, in which Annie has promised to teach them some basic moves.

Now answer Numbers 18 through 22 on your Answer Sheet. Base your answers on the passage "Beginner's Mind."

18 Most of this passage takes place in

　　F. Felicia's home in the city.

　　G. a practice hall at a martial arts camp.

　　H. a dining hall at a Tae Kwon Do camp.

　　I. a sleeping cabin at a martial arts camp.

19 Why does Felicia's excitement disappear when she finally arrives at camp?

　　A. She has begun to lose interest in martial arts.

　　B. The other campers all know each other and ignore Felicia.

　　C. She discovers that many of the other campers are not beginners like her.

　　D. She realizes that practicing martial arts is much harder than she expected.

20 Read this dictionary entry.

> **series** (seer´-eez) *noun*
>
> 1. a sequence, or group of related events, coming one after the other in succession
> 2. a number of games, contests, or sporting events played by the same two teams
> 3. a set of successive volumes of a publication, with similar subjects and formats
> 4. a set of television programs of a particular kind, as a comedy series

Read this excerpt from the passage.

> **"We will begin today with a stretching demonstration. Stretching is one of the most important parts of practice, and this series of stretches will begin each practice session."**

Which meaning best fits the way the word *series* is used in the sentence above?

F. meaning 1

G. meaning 2

H. meaning 3

I. meaning 4

21 Which of the following best describes how Felicia changes from the beginning to the end of the passage?

A. She learns many moves that she didn't know.

B. She becomes good friends with the other campers.

C. She begins to relax and feel like she belongs at camp.

D. She realizes that she has more experience than she thought.

22 Which is a theme of this passage?

F. Hard exercise creates strong bodies.

G. Martial arts are a means of self-defense.

H. A change of scene can make all the difference.

I. Feeling like you are part of a group can improve self-confidence.

Read the passage "Keeping Cool with Crickets" before answering Numbers 23 through 28.

Keeping Cool with Crickets

by Lois Jacobson
illustarted by Karen Ritz

"Konnichiwa. Good Afternoon," my Japanese neighbor called through the door. "I have brought a present to welcome you to Japan."

The package was very small and tied with delicately curled ribbons. What could such a tiny box contain? Puzzled, I lifted the lid, and there, nestled in whisper-thin tissue paper, was a blue-and-white dish. It was shaped like a miniature bottle cap, and its cracked, glazed surface made it look very old—and very special.

"It's a water dish for crickets." My new friend's voice almost chirped with delight.

"What does one do with a water dish for crickets?" I asked.

"You put it inside a cricket house."

"Cricket house?"

"If you are going to live in Tokyo during the heat of the summer," said my neighbor, "you must learn to keep cool with crickets!"

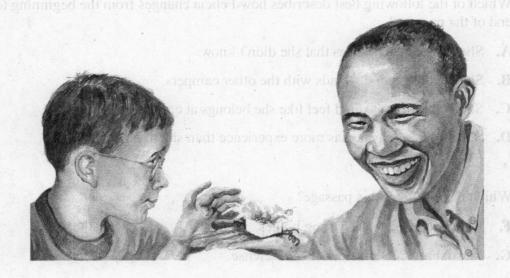

Now I was curious. I soon learned that in the Far East, people have kept crickets as pets for centuries. In the past they housed them in cages made of bamboo or delicately carved jade, which they hung from the eaves or porches of their weathered homes. Bamboo cages are still used today, but most children keep their crickets in plastic cages the colors of cool lime or raspberry sherbet[1].

During the hot, breathless summer months, Japanese parks are filled with laughing children and parents, armed with butterfly nets and small towels, pursuing their prey. The crickets are hard to catch because their hind legs are well developed for jumping. But once trapped in a net or under a small towel, they can be put in cages or small glass jars with air holes in the lids.

For people who can't catch their own, there are cricket vendors. I soon found myself at a market stall eyeing a plump, brownish black cricket. The vendor put my selection in a cardboard container. From the vibrations, I knew that my cricket didn't like being shut up inside. He needed a house.

He and I scouted out the local cricket real-estate market. Our search ended in a cluttered stall filled with bamboo wares. Tucked in a corner, amid baskets and flower containers, was a miniature Japanese house made of slender bamboo reeds. It was just right for the antique water dish—and, of course, for my cricket.

Using many hand gestures, the kimono[2]-clad shopkeeper explained that the bottom of the house must be layered with just enough soil to anchor the filled water dish. Crickets, she added, love raw potatoes, cucumbers, bits of water-soaked bread, and leafy greens—all in cricket-size portions.

Charlie and I were eager to move in. I knew he was a Charlie because only male crickets chirp. Crickets have four wings that lie flat, one pair over the other on top of their bodies. By raising the upper pair of wings and rubbing one wing over the other, the males produce their singing or chirping sound.

---

[1] **sherbet:** a frozen dessert made of fruit juice, water, sugar, and milk

[2] **kimono:** a long, loose, wide-sleeved Japanese robe

Name _____ Date _____

Each song has a meaning. Some serve as calling songs to attract females, others as courting songs. In Japan it is said that they sing, *"Kata sase suso sase samusa ga kuruzo,"* or "Sew your sleeves, sew your skirts, the cold weather is coming."

Charlie Cricket was quiet as I put down a thin layer of dirt in his home, stocked his pantry with lettuce and potatoes, and added the antique water dish. Now, how was I going to get that bundle of energy from carton to house? I lifted the cardboard flap, and Charlie eyed me, ready to do battle. Using all ten fingers, a soothing voice, and lots of encouragement, I soon had him safely in his house.

Tired from the summer heat, I hung Charlie from the eaves on the balcony. Nearby, wind chimes tinkled melodiously with each gentle breeze.

"Cool me off," I pleaded. "Chirp, Charlie, chirp." The heat hung suspended around me. And Charlie chirped! The garden bells tinkled in accompaniment. It was as if the enchanting sounds and the whirring of cricket wings awakened the air and stirred it about me ever so gently.

"Sing, Charlie!" His song sounded like the clinking of ice cubes in chilled crystal goblets. The heat seemed to waft[3] away. I had learned the Japanese art of keeping cool with crickets.

[3] **waft:** float easily or gently, as on the air

Now answer Numbers 23 through 28 on your Answer Sheet. Base your answers on the passage "Keeping Cool with Crickets."

23 The narrator of this passage is

　　A. new to Japan.

　　B. afraid of crickets.

　　C. a Japanese citizen.

　　D. suspicious of customs.

24 Read this sentence from the passage.

> **Puzzled, I lifted the lid, and there, nestled in whisper-thin tissue paper, was a blue-and-white dish.**

In the sentence above, the author uses the phrase whisper-thin to

　　F. imply that the tissue paper crumples soundlessly.

　　G. emphasize the delicate quality of the tissue paper.

　　H. show how well the tissue paper conceals the dish.

　　I. highlight how carefully the package has been wrapped.

25 Read this sentence from the passage.

> **The vendor put my selection in a cardboard container.**

What does the word *vendor* mean in the sentence above?

　　A. a person who sells things

　　B. a person who raises animals

　　C. a person who instructs others

　　D. a person who works in a manual trade

Name _____ Date _____

26 The narrator acquires a cricket by

   F. catching one in a net.

   G. receiving one as a gift.

   H. buying one in a market.

   I. finding one on the balcony.

27 Read this excerpt from the passage.

> **In Japan it is said that they sing,** *"Kata sase suso sase samusa ga kuruzo,"* **or "Sew your sleeves, sew your skirts, the cold weather is coming."**

The author includes the song line above to show that the narrator

   A. can speak Japanese fluently.

   B. is learning about Japanese culture.

   C. has lots of experience handling crickets.

   D. understands the meaning of crickets' sounds.

28 Which sentence from the passage contains figurative language?

   F. "Each song has a meaning."

   G. "The heat seemed to waft away."

   H. "His song sounded like the clinking of ice cubes in chilled crystal goblets."

   I. "The crickets are hard to catch because their hind legs are well developed for jumping."

Read the articles "The American Bald Eagle: A Recovery Success Story" and "Bald Eagle Lookout Report" before answering Numbers 29 through 35.

The American Bald Eagle: A Recovery Success Story

In 1782, the bald eagle—the only eagle native to North America—was adopted as the national bird and the symbol of the United States. Even so, in the one hundred and seventy years that followed, this marvelous bird was brought to near extinction. Wildlife experts believe that, in 1800, there were as many as 100,000 nesting eagles in America. By 1963, there were only 417 eagle pairs left in the lower forty-eight states. Today, due to recovery efforts, the number of eagle pairs exceeds 9,000. Why did the eagle population drop, and how did it bounce back so dramatically?

As the country grew and people moved further west, the eagles' world changed. People usually settled first along rivers and near lakes, disturbing the eagles' nesting places. People outnumbered eagles and took over the food supply. They saw eagles as a threat to their own animals and killed the birds on sight. Also, many eagles were killed in traps meant for wolves, or they died from lead poisoning after eating small animals killed with lead shot.

By 1940, the eagle population was dangerously low. People recognized that something had to be done or the bird would disappear altogether. In that year, Congress passed the Bald Eagle Protection Act, which made it illegal to kill eagles. Also, during the 1940s and 1950s, many dams and reservoirs were built to give energy and water supplies to people. This had the fortunate side effect of providing good eagle nesting sites, which allowed the eagle population to slowly grow.

Then, a new threat to eagles arrived: DDT, a chemical used to kill off mosquitoes and insects that attack crops. Rains washed DDT into rivers and lakes where it was absorbed by water plants and animals. Fish ate the poison-carrying plants and animals, and eagles ate those fish. DDT did not kill eagles directly; instead, it affected their ability to make strong shells for their eggs. Fewer and fewer eggs survived or hatched.

Congress recognized that there was a problem with the eagle population and listed the bald eagle as endangered on March 11, 1967. It soon became clear that the eagles had to be protected from DDT. It was banned in 1973. Congress then wrote the Endangered Species Act. This law lists animals and plants as either threatened or endangered. Listed as threatened means that they are in danger but not likely to disappear, while endangered animals and plants are likely to disappear. The act also gives the government the power to protect these animals and plants.

99

The U.S. Fish and Wildlife Service divided the country into five eagle recovery regions. Each region wrote its own recovery plan. It also set eagle population goals. Plans included programs in which bald eagles were hatched and then placed in the wild, protecting the places where bald eagles were seen nesting from development, and teaching people about the eagles. These programs were a success, and by 1995, the eagle population goals were met. The bald eagle was taken off the endangered list. While the bald eagle now flies over much of the United States, it will still be protected so that the population can continue to grow.

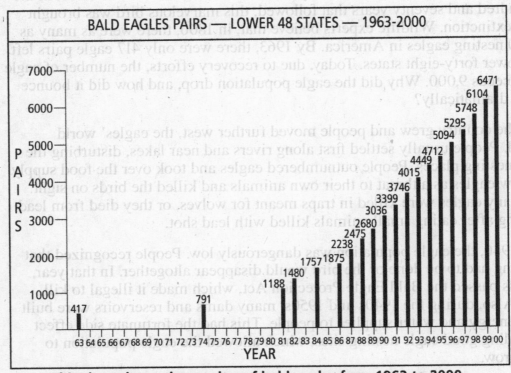

BALD EAGLES PAIRS — LOWER 48 STATES — 1963-2000

This chart shows the number of bald eagles from 1963 to 2000.
No data was available for some years.

Elmira State Park Newsletter

Bald Eagle Lookout Report by Ranger Nadia

June 2011

I have some exciting news to report, straight from the towering treetops of Elmira State Park. A bald eagle nestling has successfully returned to its nest after its first full-fledged flight. Why is this so significant? It means this nestling is well on its way to becoming another strong, healthy member of our bald eagle population. Perhaps even more significant, this nestling is a product of the first successful bald eagle nest at Elmira for decades—maybe even a century. Like much of the United States, bald eagles soaring amongst the treetops and nose-diving into the lake were once common sights in Elmira's forests. By the 1960s, however, they had virtually disappeared. They had become victims of logging practices, hunting, and pollution.

For the past five years, Elmira has seen a small but steady increase in the number of adult bald eagles making their homes in our treetops. Until this year, however, none of the eagles had laid eggs. Since January, we have been watching the nesting activities of a pair of eagles in a Red Maple on the south end of the lake. Knowing what a critical, highly-sensitive time the nest-building and egg-laying periods are for bald eagles, we were careful to keep a safe distance. We did not want to disturb the pair. The pair took turns incubating the single egg and hunting. In early April, Ranger Mario and I cheered silently from our hidden lookout point. Though we didn't have an aerial view of the nest, it appeared that the egg had hatched. The eagle pair was feeding the nestling!

As part of our region's bald eagle recovery plan, Ranger Mario and I have been observing Elmira's bald eagle activity for the past five years. We keep detailed records of our bald eagle population and their feeding (and recently, breeding!) habits. We map the locations of each nest and roosting site. In addition, we monitor the birds' overall habitat. We want to ensure that Elmira is doing everything in its power to remain a safe environment where bald eagles— and their young—can thrive.

Beginning this summer, Elmira rangers are going to be working with a team of biologists from the local university. We are going to "band" Elmira's bald eagle contingent with radio and satellite transmitters. The project is part of a larger state project to track the birds. Personally, I am very excited to participate in such an effort. Elmira doesn't have the resources to perform such close monitoring. By partnering with the university, we will be able to collect essential information about the birds' activity, movement, and survival. This type of data is so valuable in helping us learn more about Elmira's bald eagles. It is even more valuable now that one of our pairs has successfully produced offspring. The overall goal of this state project is to help bald eagles establish more nests and, ideally, more nest*lings!* The more we know about these incredible birds, the more we can protect the future of our bald eagles. And that future looks increasingly bright!

Until next time,

Ranger Nadia

Name _____ Date _____

Now answer Numbers 29 through 35 on your Answer Sheet. Base your answers on the articles "The American Bald Eagle: A Recovery Success Story" and "Bald Eagle Lookout Report."

29 Which of the following best describes how the text structure of the second and third paragraphs of the article "The American Bald Eagle: A Recovery Success Story" contributes to the development of the author's central idea?

   A. The author uses comparison-contrast to help readers distinguish past and current bald eagle populations in the U.S.

   B. The author uses problem-solution to show how the Bald Eagle Protection Act solved the declining bald eagle population.

   C. The author uses a sequence of events to help readers understand the events that led to the recovery of the bald eagle population.

   D. The author uses cause-and-effect to show how the population of bald eagles in the U.S. first began to decline and temporarily recover.

30 Based on the information and the chart in the article "The American Bald Eagle: A Recovery Success Story," which conclusion can the reader draw about bald eagle populations between 1963 and 2000?

   F. The most dramatic rise in the population of bald eagles occurred between 1963 and 1974.

   G. The population of bald eagles began to recover significantly after DDT was banned in 1973.

   H. The population of bald eagles was steadily declining until Congress listed the bald eagle as endangered in 1967.

   I. After bald eagle population goals were met in 1995, the bald eagle population remained steady, neither increasing nor decreasing.

31 Read this sentence from the article "Bald Eagle Lookout Report."

> **Though we didn't have an aerial view of the nest, it appeared that the egg had hatched.**

What does the word *aerial* mean in the sentence above?

   A. close-up

   B. focused

   C. overhead

   D. personal

Name _____ Date _____

32 Read this sentence from the article "Bald Eagle Lookout Report."

> **We want to ensure that Elmira is doing everything in its power to remain a safe environment where bald eagles—and their young—can thrive.**

What does the word *ensure* mean in the sentence above?

F. attempt

G. suggest

H. make certain

I. make a promise

33 The overall tone of the article "Bald Eagle Lookout Report" can best be described as

A. hopeful.

B. humorous.

C. persuasive.

D. sharp.

34 What information do both the articles "The American Bald Eagle: A Recovery Success Story" and "Bald Eagle Lookout Report" discuss?

F. how the Endangered Species Act protects bald eagles

G. some of the factors that led to declining bald eagle populations

H. a program in which bald eagles are hatched and then placed into the wild

I. why it is so important to close-monitor bald eagles and collect data on them

35 How do the author's approaches to the information about bald eagles in the articles "The American Bald Eagle: A Recovery Success Story" and "Bald Eagle Lookout Report" differ?

A. The author of "The American Bald Eagle: A Recovery Success Story" presents information in a research report, giving the history of bald eagles. The author of "Bald Eagle Lookout Report" presents information through an interview with a ranger.

B. The author of "The American Bald Eagle: A Recovery Success Story" presents information in a persuasive article, convincing audiences to help protect bald eagles. The author of "Bald Eagle Lookout Report" narrates a story about a ranger observing bald eagles.

C. The author of "The American Bald Eagle: A Recovery Success Story" presents information in an explanatory article, telling how bald eagles can be protected. The author of "Bald Eagle Lookout Report" reports her experiences working with bald eagles in a scientific journal.

D. The author of "The American Bald Eagle: A Recovery Success Story" presents information objectively, explaining why the bald eagle population declined and then recovered. The author of "Bald Eagle Lookout Report" gives a first-hand account of her experiences observing bald eagles in a park.

Revising and Editing

Read the introduction and the article "A Canyon That's Grand" before answering Numbers 1 through 7.

Mikaela wrote this article after visiting the Grand Canyon. Read her article and think about the changes she should make.

A Canyon That's Grand

(1) Each year, almost five million people travel to Arizona to visit the Grand Canyon National Park, and there's a good reason for this popularity.

(2) Because of its big big size and breathtaking beauty, the Grand Canyon is one of the seven natural wonders of the world. (3) The Great Barrier Reef is another natural wonder of the world.

(4) Over the ages, the rushing waters of the Colorado River have slowly cut through the sandstone and limestone rock, creating the 277-mile-long gorge known as the Grand Canyon. (5) The Colorado River separates the two sides of the park into the North Rim and the South Rim. (6) Standing on one side of the canyon. (7) You can see the river about one mile below. (8) The canyon may be deep, but it is wide, too. (9) In some places, the span between the two sides is about 15 miles!

(10) As part of their explorashon, many people want to hike from one side of the canyon to the other. (11) In order to do so, they can walk across a narrow bridge that is 70 feet above the River. (12) Hikers begin the 21-mile trek at the top of the canyon (called the rim), climb down the canyon, cross the bridge, and climb up the other side.

(13) If you visit the Grand Canyon, remember to bring a camera to capture the spectacular scenes? (14) The scenery will appear to transform before your eyes as the sun rises and sets. (15) The hue of the canyon's rocky walls changes from brown to pink to orange. (16) Observe the dramatic waterfalls and fascinating wildlife. (17) Photograph the dramatic waterfalls and fascinating wildlife. (18) You will absolutely be amazed, and so will the people who look at your photographs.

Now answer Numbers 1 through 7 on your Answer Sheet. Base your answers on the changes Mikaela should make.

1   What change should be made in sentence 2?

    A. change *big big* to **massive**

    B. insert a comma after *size*

    C. delete the comma after *beauty*

    D. change *is* to **are**

2   What revision is needed in sentences 6 and 7?

    F. Standing about one mile below the canyon, you can see the river on one side.

    G. Standing on one side of the canyon, you can see the river about one mile below.

    H. When you stand on one side of the canyon and you can see the river about one mile below.

    I. Standing on one side of the canyon you can see the river about one mile below the canyon.

Name _____ Date _____

3 What change should be made in sentence 10?

    A. change *explorashon* to **exploration**

    B. change *want* to **wanted**

    C. change *hike* to **hiked**

    D. change *canyon* to **Canyon**

4 What change should be made in sentence 11?

    F. delete the comma after *so*

    G. change *can walk* to **walks**

    H. change *feet* to **foot**

    I. change *River* to **river**

5 What change should be made in sentence 13?

    A. change the comma to a period

    B. change *bring* to **brought**

    C. change *scenes* to **sceans**

    D. change the question mark to a period

6 What is the best way to combine sentences 16 and 17?

    F. Observe the dramatic waterfalls, photograph the fascinating wildlife.

    G. Observe the dramatic waterfalls and photograph the fascinating wildlife.

    H. Observe, photograph the dramatic waterfalls and the fascinating wildlife.

    I. Observe and photograph the dramatic waterfalls and the fascinating wildlife.

7 Which sentence does NOT belong in this article?

    A. sentence 3

    B. sentence 5

    C. sentence 9

    D. sentence 12

Read the introduction and the passage "Books for All" before answering
Numbers 8 through 14.

*Juan wrote a passage about an event he'll remember for a long time. Read
his passage and think about the changes he should make.*

Books for All

(1) An article in the newspaper I read about our town library's limited
availability of children's books. (2) This immediately caused me concern, as
reading is one of my favorite pastimes. (3) I had already read my own books
several times, so what would I do this summer with few books available to
read? (4) Reading is one of my favorite pastimes. (5) That's when the idea
occurred to me: I could start a book exchange! (6) I placed a few phone
calls and soon had my friends on-board, ready to help me implement a plan.

(7) Collaborating with our town's library, we organized a community
book exchange. (8) My friends and I posted notices about the exchange
around town, inviting all children to bring books to the library to trade.
(9) The next Saturday morning, a line of over 50 children and their
parents stand outside the library!

(10) My friends and I got to work immediately. (11) In a spare room in
the library, we collected the books, distributing to people a ticket for each
book they were exchanging. (12) Once the books assembled, a person
could redeem a ticket for a book. (13) While the exchangers waited and
chatted about their favorite books, my friends and I organized the books
on shelfs according to genre and age-appropriateness. (14) By the end of
the day, more than 200 people had passed through, but they all left with
books to read over the summer.

Name _____   Date _____

(15) A parent of one of the children who attended happened to be

a reporter for the local newspaper. (16) She was so impressed with our

efforts that she took our picture and wrote an article about us. (17) I was

proud that I was able to help my fellow book lovers, and I was happy to

have new storys to read! (18) I will save the article in a scrapbook and use

it to inspire other kids to find ways to help their communities.

_____

Now answer Numbers 8 through 14 on your Answer Sheet. Base your answers on the changes Juan should make.

8 What is the best way to revise sentence 1?

   F. I read an article in the newspaper about our town library's limited availability of children's books.

   G. An article I read in the newspaper about our town library's limited availability of children's books.

   H. I read in the newspaper, article, about our town library's limited availability of children's books.

   I. An article in the newspaper about our town library's limited availability of children's books I read.

9 What change should be made in sentence 9?

   A. delete the comma after *morning*

   B. change *line* to **lines**

   C. insert a comma after *children*

   D. change *stand* to **stood**

Name _____ Date _____

10 What change should be made in sentence 12?

   F. change *books* to **book**

   G. insert **were** before *assembled*

   H. change *redeem* to **redeemed**

   I. insert a comma after *ticket*

11 What change should be made in sentence 13?

   A. change *chatted* to **chatting**

   B. change *organized* to **organised**

   C. change *shelfs* to **shelves**

   D. change the period to an exclamation point

12 What revision is needed in sentence 14?

   F. change *had passed* to **passing**

   G. delete the comma after *through*

   H. change *but* to **and**

   I. change *left* to **leaving**

13 What change should be made in sentence 17?

   A. change *was proud* to **were proud**

   B. change *my* to **mine**

   C. change *and* to **but**

   D. change *storys* to **stories**

14 Which sentence does NOT belong in this passage?

   F. sentence 4

   G. sentence 8

   H. sentence 11

   I. sentence 16

Read the introduction and the article "A Gem of a Story" before answering
Numbers 15 through 20.

*Kathryn wrote this article about a new book she read. Read her article
and think about the changes she should make.*

A Gem of a Story

(1) *Discovering the Shore,* published by Gold Leaf Books, is a new
work of fiction by Charlene Burkett. (2) The book takes place on the
Texas Gulf Coast. (3) It follows the main character, Matt, so that he
discovers life by the sea.

(4) The book begins as Matt travels from his home in the Texas
Panhandle to the Texas Coast to visit his grandmother. (5) During the long
car ride, he makes it clear to their parents that he would have preferred to
spend summer vacation at home.

(6) Once him arrives at the coast, Matt's mood begins to change little by
little. (7) Having never been to the beach before, Matt is slowly charmed by
the sound of the waves and the sea. (8) On peaceful walks, at sunset, he and
Grandma have heartfelt comversations. (9) On one walk, swimming only
a few yards away from the shore, Grandma points out dolphins. (10) By
the end of the summer, Matt is hesitant to return home. (11) He has a new
admiration for his grandmother and he has discovered a love for the ocean.

(12) Burkett's writing is descriptive, especially when she portrays
life by the ocean's shore. (13) The plot is moving and the characters are
realistic. (14) Readers will grow to love the coast just as Matt does, and
they will cheer as he grows closer to his grandmother. (15) Burkett has
given us a sparkling gem of a story!

Now answer Numbers 15 through 20 on your Answer Sheet. Base your answers on the changes Kathryn should make.

15 What change should be made in sentence 3?

    A. change *follows* to **was following**

    B. change *character* to **charactar**

    C. change *so that* to **while**

    D. change *sea* to **Sea**

16 What change should be made in sentence 5?

    F. delete the comma after *ride*

    G. change *their* to **his**

    H. change *preferred* to **prefered**

    I. change *spend* to **spending**

17 What revision should be made in sentence 6?

    A. change *him* to **he**

    B. change *arrives* to **had arrived**

    C. change *Matt's* to **Matts'**

    D. change the period to an exclamation point

18 What change should be made in sentence 8?

    F. delete the comma after *walks*

    G. change *have* to **has**

    H. change *comversations* to **conversations**

    I. change the period to a question mark

19 What is the best way to revise sentence 9?

   A. On one walk, Grandma points out dolphins swimming only a few yards away from the shore.

   B. On one walk, dolphins Grandma points out swimming only a few yards away from the shore.

   C. Swimming only a few yards away from the shore, on one walk Grandma points out dolphins.

   D. Swimming dolphins Grandma points out on one walk, only a few yards away from the shore.

20 What change should be made in sentence 11?

   F. change *admiration* to **admirion**

   G. insert a comma after *grandmother*

   H. change *love* to **loves**

   I. change *ocean* to **Ocean**

Name _____ Date _____

Writing to Explain

Read the prompt and plan your response.

Most people have goals that they are working toward.

Think about a goal that you are working toward.

Now write to explain why you set this goal and how you are working toward it.

Planning Page

Use this space to make your notes before you begin writing. The writing on this page will NOT be scored.

_____

_____

_____

_____

_____

_____

_____

_____

_____

_____

_____

_____

Begin writing your response here. The writing on this page and the next page
WILL be scored.

_____

_____

_____

_____

_____

_____

_____

_____

_____

_____

_____

_____

_____

_____

_____

_____

_____

_____

_____

_____

_____

_____

_____

Reading Complex Text

Read the passage "The Flight" and the poem "Unflappable Boy." As you read, stop and answer each question. Use evidence from the passage and the poem to support your answers.

The Flight

from *Peter Pan* by J.M. Barrie

In this excerpt from the book Peter Pan, *three children named Wendy, John, and Michael, are flying with Peter Pan and his companion, Tink. They are on their way to a magical place called Neverland.*

"Second to the right, and straight on till morning."

That, Peter had told Wendy, was the way to the Neverland; but even birds, carrying maps and consulting them at windy corners, could not have sighted it with these instructions. Peter, you see, just said anything that came into his head.

At first his companions trusted him implicitly, and so great were the delights of flying that they wasted time circling round church spires or any other tall objects on the way that took their fancy.

John and Michael raced, Michael getting a start.

They recalled with contempt that not so long ago they had thought themselves fine fellows for being able to fly round a room.

Not so long ago. But how long ago? They were flying over the sea before this thought began to disturb Wendy seriously. John thought it was their second sea and their third night.

Sometimes it was dark and sometimes light, and now they were very cold and again too warm. Did they really feel hungry at times, or were they merely pretending, because Peter had such a jolly new way of feeding them? His way was to pursue birds who had food in their mouths suitable for humans and snatch it from them; then the birds would follow and snatch it back; and they would all go chasing each other gaily for miles, parting at last with mutual expressions of good-will. But Wendy noticed with gentle concern that Peter did not seem to know that this was rather an odd way of getting your bread and butter, nor even that there are other ways. . . .

Name _____ Date _____

1 Why does Wendy feel gentle concern for Peter?

_____

_____

_____

When playing follow my leader, Peter would fly close to the water and touch each shark's tail in passing, just as in the street you may run your finger along an iron railing. They could not follow him in this with much success, so perhaps it was rather like showing off, especially as he kept looking behind to see how many tails they missed.

"You must be nice to him," Wendy impressed on her brothers. "What could we do if he were to leave us!"

"We could go back," Michael said.

"How could we ever find our way back without him?"

"Well, then, we could go on," said John.

"That is the awful thing, John. We should have to go on, for we don't know how to stop."

This was true, Peter had forgotten to show them how to stop.

John said that if the worst came to the worst, all they had to do was to go straight on, for the world was round, and so in time they must come back to their own window.

"And who is to get food for us, John?"

"I nipped a bit out of that eagle's mouth pretty neatly, Wendy."

"After the twentieth try," Wendy reminded him. "And even though we became good at picking up food, see how we bump against clouds and things if he is not near to give us a hand."

Indeed they were constantly bumping. They could now fly strongly, though they still kicked far too much; but if they saw a cloud in front of them, the more they tried to avoid it, the more certainly did they bump into it. If Nana had been with them, she would have had a bandage round Michael's forehead by this time.

Peter was not with them for the moment, and they felt rather lonely up there by themselves. He could go so much faster than they that he would suddenly shoot out of sight, to have some adventure in which they had no share. He would come down laughing over something fearfully funny he had been saying to a star, but he had already forgotten what it was, or he would come up with mermaid scales still sticking to him, and yet not be able to say for certain what had been happening. It was really rather irritating to children who had never seen a mermaid. . . .

[T]o make amends he showed them how to lie out flat on a strong wind that was going their way, and this was such a pleasant change that they tried it several times and found that they could sleep thus with security. Indeed they would have slept longer, but Peter tired quickly of sleeping, and soon he would cry in his captain voice, "We get off here." So with occasional tiffs, but on the whole rollicking, they drew near the Neverland; for after many moons they did reach it, and, what is more, they had been going pretty straight all the time, not perhaps so much owing to the guidance of Peter or Tink as because the island was looking for them. It is only thus that any one may sight those magic shores.

"There it is," said Peter calmly.

"Where, where?"

"Where all the arrows are pointing."

Indeed a million golden arrows were pointing it out to the children, all directed by their friend the sun, who wanted them to be sure of their way before leaving them for the night.

Wendy and John and Michael stood on tip-toe in the air to get their first sight of the island. Strange to say, they all recognized it at once, and until fear fell upon them they hailed it, not as something long dreamt of and seen at last, but as a familiar friend to whom they were returning home for the holidays.

---

2 Why does the author describe Neverland as a *familiar friend*?

_____

_____

_____

Unflappable Boy

The boy and his dog on a bed of green grass
Looked up at the sapphire sky,
And the clouds seemed to call, and the wind seemed to whisper,
"Come on! Spread your wings! You can fly!"

The boy spread his arms like an eagle in flight,
While the dog cheered him on with his tail,
And he imagined he rose o'er the tops of the trees
With the wind at his back like a sail!

(Now the trouble with arms is they're missing the feathers,
And their bones are all filled with marrow
Which makes them too heavy to soar in the clouds
Like a bluebird, a finch, or a sparrow.)

3 Why does the author use parentheses in the section above?

_____

_____

_____

So the unflappable boy flapped his featherless wings,
But no closer he got toward the sun,
So the dog-tired boy and boy-tired dog built their nest
In the grass and had fun.

4 Tell how the characters' experience of flying in "The Flight" differs from the boy's experience of flying in "Unflappable Boy."

_____

_____

_____

_____

_____

Reading and Analyzing Text

Read the article "An Ancient People" before answering Numbers 1 through 17.

An Ancient People

Over the years, scientists have unearthed many exciting secrets of an ancient people. Clues left behind show that these people were advanced in many fields. They built majestic pyramids and huge cities, they developed a system of numbers and a written language, and through art and writing, they left records of their history. The tombs of their kings were filled with priceless treasures for use in the afterlife. In many ways, this civilization was similar to that of the ancient Egyptians, but it was a world away. This was the civilization of the ancient Mayas in Central America.

Pyramids

Mayans built pyramids in many parts of Central America. Like all pyramids, they are large at the bottom and small at the top. Unlike many Egyptian pyramids, the Mayan structures have sides like the steps of a staircase; while the steps are too steep to be used as stairs, they may have had other purposes. The pattern of steps on one pyramid seems to represent the seasons and the days of the year. Shadows cast on the steps change throughout the year. These changes show the movement of the sun through the seasons. The Mayans designed the pyramid so that it gives a remarkable sign twice a year, only when the sun is directly overhead at the equator. On those days, the shadow of a snake appears to climb or descend the steps!

Pyramids that stood up to twenty stories tall were at the heart of every Mayan city. Their towering presence was meant to serve as a reminder of the greatness of Mayan rulers.

Calendars

The Mayans excelled in astronomy and math and invented a number system based on the number twenty. The Mayans had the distinction of using the concept of zero long before most other cultures did. Mayans charted the movements of objects in the night sky in great detail and came to understand that the movements were cyclical. This knowledge led them to create elaborate calendars which plotted the movement of stars and planets with great accuracy; in fact, they can still be used today to predict the dates of eclipses[1]!

Writing

The Mayans developed one of the earliest written languages. Their writings have been found on stone tablets and pottery. They also wrote in books made of tree bark, but most of the books have been lost. Like the Egyptians, Mayans used pictures as letters. The letters are part of a complex system of writing. For a long time, it was too hard for experts to understand because some symbols stand for a whole word while others stand for just one syllable. Also, the symbols to spell a word can be arranged in different ways. In recent years, experts have finally broken the code, and they can now read the Mayan writings. Most praise Mayan kings and their belief in many gods or tell highlights of Mayan history.

Art

The Mayans used art to show respect for their gods and rulers. Likenesses of these figures were carved in stone high on buildings. Their stone faces are mysterious and commanding. Thrones carved of stone often showed the king sitting with gods. Some carvings show rulers with their heirs or ancestors while others depict them waging war or conquering enemies. The king's daily life was also shown in art. Scenes painted on pots show kings at feasts and celebrations.

Mayans believed art and beauty were important in the afterlife. For that reason, they placed fine works of art such as statues, jade masks, and jewelry in Mayan tombs.

Recently, carvings and statues have been discovered in underground temples built inside a labyrinth of caves. Experts wonder whether the Mayans used the temples as burial places. That is just one of the mysteries of the Mayans that is still waiting to be solved!

[1] **eclipses:** the partial or complete obscuring of one celestial body by another

Now answer Numbers 1 through 17 on your Answer Sheet. Base your answers on the article "An Ancient People."

1 What is the main idea of the first paragraph of the article?

    A. The Mayans built large pyramids and cities in ancient times.

    B. The Mayans built a great civilization similar to that of the ancient Egyptians.

    C. Scientists have found clues that show that the Mayans had a written language.

    D. The Mayans believed the treasures they put in tombs would be used in the afterlife.

2 Read this sentence from the article.

> **They built majestic pyramids and huge cities, they developed a system of numbers and a written language, and through art and writing, they left records of their history.**

What does the word *majestic* mean in the sentence above?

    F. puzzling

    G. simple

    H. splendid

    I. unusual

3 Read this sentence from the article.

> **The tombs of their kings were filled with priceless treasures for use in the afterlife.**

Which word has the same sound as the underlined letter in *treasures* in the sentence above?

    A. collision

    B. fizzy

    C. smashing

    D. unsure

Name _____ Date _____

4 Read this sentence from the article.

> **The tombs of their kings were filled with priceless treasures for use in the afterlife.**

What does the word *priceless* mean in the sentence above?

F. of unknown value

G. without much value

H. having a secret price

I. too valuable for a price

5 Mayan pyramids were different from many Egyptian pyramids in that they were

A. erected in ancient times.

B. small, well-hidden structures.

C. large at the bottom and small at the top.

D. built with sides that looked like stair steps.

6 Which fact supports the author's opinion that the Mayans liked to create dramatic effects with their structures?

F. They began using zero before most other cultures.

G. They used astronomy to help them create accurate calendars.

H. They created the illusion of a snake crawling on the pyramid steps.

I. They used some symbols to represent a whole word and others to represent one syllable.

7 Read this sentence from the article.

> **The Mayans designed the pyramid so that it gives a remarkable sign twice a year. . . .**

Which word has the same suffix as the word *remarkable* in the sentence above?

A. dabble

B. label

C. likeable

D. stable

8 Read this sentence from the article.

> **The Mayans excelled in astronomy and math and invented a number system based on the number twenty.**

What does the word *astronomy* mean in the sentence above?

F. the study of ancient civilizations

G. the study of time and its measurement

H. the study of numbers and their relationships

I. the study of objects and matter in outer space

9 Read this sentence from the article.

> **The Mayans had the distinction of using the concept of zero long before most other cultures did.**

Which word belongs to the same word family as the word *distinction* in the sentence above?

A. disclose

B. distance

C. distinguish

D. distribute

10 Read this sentence from the article.

> **Mayans charted the movements of objects in the night sky in great detail and came to understand that the movements were cyclical.**

What does the word *cyclical* mean in the sentence above?

F. random

G. rapid

H. remarkable

I. repeating

11 Read this sentence from the article.

> **This knowledge led them to create elaborate calendars which plotted the movement of stars and planets with great accuracy; in fact, they can still be used today to predict the dates of eclipses!**

What does the word *elaborate* mean in the sentence above?

A. beautiful

B. complex

C. delicate

D. simple

12 What similarity between Egyptian and Mayan writing is mentioned in the article?

F. Both use pictures as letters.

G. Both are decorated by extra pictures.

H. Both use one symbol for each syllable.

I. Both have several spellings for the same word.

⓭ Which sentence from the article states the main idea of the section *Art*?

   A. "The Mayans used art to show respect for their gods and rulers."

   B. "Some carvings show rulers with their heirs or ancestors while others depict them waging war or conquering enemies."

   C. "Thrones carved of stone often showed the king sitting with gods."

   D. "The king's daily life was also shown in art."

⓮ Which of the following statements in the article is an opinion?

   F. "Their stone faces are mysterious and commanding."

   G. "Mayans believed art and beauty were important in the afterlife."

   H. "Likenesses of these figures were carved in stone high on buildings."

   I. "Recently, carvings and statues have been discovered in underground temples built inside a labyrinth of caves."

⓯ Read this sentence from the article.

> **Some carvings show rulers with their heirs or ancestors while others depict them waging war or conquering enemies.**

What does the word *depict* mean in the sentence above?

   A. divide

   B. entertain

   C. imitate

   D. show

⓰ Which detail supports the idea that Mayans believed art was important in the afterlife?

   F. Mayan scribes added artwork to their writings.

   G. Mayan kings were buried with beautiful works of art.

   H. Mayans decorated pottery with pictures of the king's daily life.

   I. Mayans put stone likenesses of kings and gods on their buildings.

Name _____ Date _____

17 Read this sentence from the article.

Experts wonder whether the Mayans used the temples as burial places.

What is the correct way to divide the word *burial* into syllables in the
sentence above?

    A. bur • ial

    B. bur • i • al

    C. bu • ria • l

    D. bur • ia • l

Read the passage "The Stonecutter's Wish" before answering Numbers 18 through 35.

The Stonecutter's Wish

Long ago, there lived a stonecutter who made his living fashioning useful items out of rock. He chiseled everything from flat stepping stones to heavy blocks for building great houses. The stonecutter was never without customers because everyone valued his reliable skills and careful work.

One day, the stonecutter delivered stone blocks to the home of a wealthy family. The opulent home was filled with marvelous and beautiful things; finest of all was the master's luxurious bed, with elaborate carvings on its headboard and sheets of silk on its plump feather mattress.

"If only I were rich and could sleep in such a bed," lamented the stonecutter, "I would be happier than anyone in the world!"

Day after day, the stonecutter daydreamed about the elegant possessions and life of a rich man—how he wished for that life! He pictured in vivid detail the mansion he would own if he were wealthy.

Then one day, a strange and astonishing thing happened. When he returned home from work, the stonecutter discovered his modest hut had disappeared, and in its place was a mansion just like the one in his daydreams!

"What a fortunate turn of events!" cried the stonecutter. He decided to give up his occupation to enjoy his newfound prosperity. At first he was content, sitting all day in his mansion, but in time he grew restless and wandered outside to admire his gardens. The harsh summer sun burned his skin and made him feel faint. It blazed so intensely that the grounds around the mansion quickly became scorched and dried up.

The stonecutter pondered his situation. "I am wealthy and the sun hasn't a single penny," he thought. "Yet the sun can parch the life out of everything green. Its baking heat steals my strength and withers my will. If only I were the sun, I would be mightier than anything anywhere!"

The next morning another strange and astonishing thing happened. When the stonecutter awoke, he was no longer in his elegant bed in his elegant house; instead, he was high above the Earth and was filled with a fiery feeling of power. The stonecutter had become the sun!

The stonecutter, fascinated by his new self, shone his piercing rays onto the Earth, causing fields and crops to shrivel under his wilting power. People of all kinds—young, old, rich, and poor—suffered in his heat. Their faces reddened, their strength faded, and they were forced to take shelter in their homes, but the stonecutter felt no sympathy for them. Instead, he swelled with pride when he saw how everything on Earth became powerless before him. His pride lasted until one day when a soft, white cloud covered his face and gave the Earth relief. The sun had no power as long as the cloud floated in front of him.

"How is it that a cloud can stop my rays? There is no satisfaction in being the sun if I am not the greatest of all," he observed bitterly. "A cloud is the thing to be. If only I were a cloud, I would be greater than the sun, greater than anything anywhere!"

When night came and the sun sank out of sight from the land, a third strange and astonishing thing happened. The stonecutter still appeared high above the Earth, but he no longer had the sun's fiery power. Instead, he drifted through the sky with a serene, silent kind of strength. When morning came, he saw his great shadow moving over the ground. The stonecutter had become the cloud!

Delighted at his transformation, the stonecutter puffed himself up larger and wider, holding back the sun's rays and sprinkling down rain to refresh everything below. His precipitation made the whole Earth green and lush again.

The stonecutter wanted to see the extent of his power so he rained and stormed with all his might. Torrents of rain overflowed rivers and flooded the land; towns, villages, and roads washed away. With satisfaction, the stonecutter surveyed the destruction he had caused. Then he noticed that one thing had remained immovable in the face of his violent storms: an immense rock on the side of the mountain.

"That rock is unaffected by my power though everything around it is flooded or destroyed!" cried the stonecutter in angry disbelief. "If only I were the rock, I would be stronger than the cloud and the sun—at last, I would be stronger than anything anywhere!"

The next morning, the stonecutter had a strange and astonishing feeling, as if he were immense and solid and strong enough to withstand any assault. The stonecutter had become the rock!

He laughed at the blazing sun and the pelting rain because nothing moved or changed him in the slightest way. Then suddenly, something small and sharp cut into him and severed a large hunk of rock that fell to the ground. The attacker

Name _____ Date _____

was a stonecutter working his trade! Though the rock had the strength to endure many things, its power was useless in resisting the hammer and chisel[1].

In indignation, the stonecutter in the rock roared, "How is it that a mere man can destroy this mightiest of rocks? If only I were a stonecutter, I would be satisfied at last!"

Then a strange, but not so astonishing, thing happened. The stonecutter awoke in his own modest bed in his modest little hut. He went back to his trade and worked hard every day, and though he had very little, he had all that he needed. Instead of longing for power and greatness, the stonecutter was satisfied with his life for he was sure he was as happy as anyone anywhere.

_____

Now answer Numbers 18 through 35 on your Answer Sheet. Base your answers on the passage "The Stonecutter's Wish."

18 The problems faced by the main character in this passage are caused by

   F. the stonecutter's lack of work.

   G. the floods that wash out his town.

   H. the character's own greed and envy.

   I. the snobbishness of a rich customer.

19 Read this sentence from the passage.

> The opulent home was filled with marvelous and beautiful things; finest of all was the master's luxurious bed, with elaborate carvings on its headboard and sheets of silk on its plump feather mattress.

What does the word *opulent* mean in the sentence above?

   A. complicated

   B. friendly

   C. luxurious

   D. sparkling

[1]**chisel:** a metal tool with a wedge-shaped blade, used to cut and shape stone

Name _____ Date _____

20 Read this sentence from the passage.

> **Day after day, the stonecutter daydreamed about the elegant**
> **possessions and life of a rich man—how he wished for that life!**

Which word belongs to the same word family as the word *possessions* in the
sentence above?

F. deposit

G. impossible

H. possessed

I. postcard

21 Read this sentence from the passage.

> **"What a fortunate turn of events!" cried the stonecutter.**

Which word has the same sounds as the underlined letters in *fortunate* in the
sentence above?

A. created

B. delicately

C. eggbeater

D. water

22 Read this sentence from the passage.

> **He decided to give up his occupation to enjoy his newfound prosperity.**

What does the word *prosperity* mean in the sentence above?

F. career

G. dwelling

H. power

I. wealth

Name _____ Date _____

23 What makes the stonecutter become dissatisfied with being a rich man?

   A. his own boredom

   B. the sun's heat

   C. his garden's ugliness

   D. the flood's destruction

24 Read this sentence from the passage.

The stonecutter pondered his situation.

What does the word *pondered* mean in the sentence above?

   F. considered

   G. explained

   H. regretted

   I. remembered

25 Read this sentence from the passage.

**Their faces reddened, their strength faded, and they were forced to take
shelter in their homes, but the stonecutter felt no sympathy for them.**

What does the word *sympathy* mean in the sentence above?

   A. joy

   B. hatred

   C. shame

   D. understanding

26 Read this sentence from the passage.

> **Instead, he swelled with pride when he saw how everything on Earth became powerless before him.**

What does the word *powerless* mean in the sentence above?

F. full of power

G. against power

H. without power

I. having more power

27 Read this sentence from the passage.

> **His pride lasted until one day when a soft, white cloud covered his face and gave the Earth relief.**

How does the setting in the sentence above affect the plot development in the passage?

A. As the sun, the stonecutter knows he can push the cloud back, keeping the earth dry and scorched.

B. Seeing the cloud reinforces the stonecutter's feelings of greatness and power in his new form, the sun.

C. The stonecutter realizes that since a cloud can overpower the sun, he now wants to become a cloud.

D. The cloud brings rain with it, making the stonecutter realize that it would be better to be once again on the lush earth.

Name _____ Date _____

28 Read this excerpt from the passage.

> **The stonecutter wanted to see the extent of his power so he rained
> and stormed with all his might. Torrents of rain overflowed the rivers
> and flooded the land; towns, villages, and roads washed away. With
> satisfaction, the stonecutter surveyed the destruction he had caused.**

The excerpt above shows that the stonecutter is

F. cautious.

G. unpredictable.

H. without mercy.

I. easily entertained.

29 Read this sentence from the passage.

> **With satisfaction, the stonecutter surveyed the destruction he
> had caused.**

Which word has the same sound as the underlined letter in *destruction* in the
sentence above?

A. fasten

B. instructing

C. pleasing

D. sugar

30 Read this sentence from the passage.

> **Then he noticed that one thing had remained immovable in the face of
> his violent storms: an immense rock on the side of the mountain.**

What does the word *immovable* mean in the sentence above?

F. moving inward

G. moving outward

H. constantly moving

I. not able to be moved

135

Name _____ Date _____

31 Read this sentence from the passage.

> **"That rock is unaffected by my power though everything around it is flooded or destroyed!" cried the stonecutter in angry disbelief.**

What is the base word for the word *disbelief* in the sentence above?

A. belief

B. bell

C. dis

D. lie

32 Read this sentence from the passage.

> **"That rock is unaffected by my power though everything around it is flooded or destroyed!" cried the stonecutter in angry disbelief.**

The author uses the words above to convey the stonecutter's

F. desire for ultimate power.

G. disappointment in himself.

H. shock at the flood's scope.

I. fury at the rock for breaking.

33 Read this excerpt from the passage.

> **Then a strange, but not so astonishing, thing happened. The stonecutter awoke in his own modest bed in his own modest little hut.**

How does the setting in the excerpt above help move the passage toward a resolution?

A. Waking up in his own home, the stonecutter figures out that will never be able to change form again.

B. By returning to his own home and his work, the stonecutter understands that he is content with the life he has.

C. As the stonecutter goes back to his work and his own home, he grows more dissatisfied with being a poor stonecutter.

D. When the stonecutter realizes that he has woken up in his own bed, he mourns the loss of his greatness but goes back to work anyway.

Name _____ Date _____

34 Why is the last paragraph of the passage important?

    F. It describes the setting of the passage.

    G. It introduces the main problem of the passage.

    H. It explains the lesson learned by the main character.

    I. It describes a flashback to an event that happened earlier.

35 The stonecutter had many customers because he was known for his careful work and his

    A. competence.

    B. competent.

    C. competently.

    D. competition.

STOP

Revising and Editing

Read the introduction and the article "A Book for Pet Lovers" before answering
Numbers 1 through 7.

*Brianna wrote this article about a book she read. Read her article and
think about the changes she should make.*

A Book for Pet Lovers

(1) *The Dog Quest* is the story of two kids who work really hardly to
get a dog. (2) The story begins with Jett and Laila begging their parents
to let them have a dog. (3) Their parents are hesitant to get a pet, though.
(4) They point out that it takes time, money, and effort to train and care for
a pet. (5) They also think a pet will cause extra messes before the house.

(6) Jett and Laila remain determined. (7) They do all they can to
address their parents' concerns. (8) First, they take on more housecleaning
chores. (9) Then, with their parents' permission and help, they start a pet-
care business. (10) They promise to use their profits to help pay for dog
food and vet bills which are no small expenses.

(11) The problems Jett and Laila have in their pet business are the
funniest parts of the book. (12) They have some incredibble mishaps with
Lars the cowardly Great Dane, Boo the disappearing snake, and Chaos
the claw-happy cat.

(13) In the end, the parents change their minds. (14) They admit that
Jett and Laila have prove they will take good care of a dog. (15) They all
go to the animal shelter together to find just the right pet. (16) The kids
use their pet-sitting experience to screen the dogs for bad habits.

(17) For those, like mine, who love animals and humorous fiction, *The Dog Quest* is a must-read book.

___

Now answer Numbers 1 through 7 on your Answer Sheet. Base your answers on the changes Brianna should make.

1 What change should be made in sentence 1?

A. change *Quest* to **quest**

B. change *work* to **working**

C. change *hardly* to **hard**

D. change *get* to **got**

2 What change should be made in sentence 5?

F. change *They* to **Them**

G. change *will* to **was**

H. change *before* to **around**

I. insert a comma after *messes*

3 What change should be made in sentence 10?

A. insert a comma after *promise*

B. change *their* to **they're**

C. insert a comma after *bills*

D. change *expenses* to **expense**

4 What change should be made in sentence 12?

  F. change *have* to **has**

  G. change *some* to **sum**

  H. change *incredibble* to **incredible**

  I. change *disappearing* to **disappearance**

5 What change should be made in sentence 14?

  A. change *admit* to **admits**

  B. change *prove* to **proven**

  C. change *good* to **well**

  D. insert a comma after *of*

6 Which sentence could best be added after sentence 16?

  F. Your local animal shelter is a good place for to find a great pet.

  G. Dogs need attention and training in order to learn how to follow commands.

  H. They talk about the time that Boo the snake hid behind the books in a bookcase.

  I. Ultimately, they choose a great mixed-breed dog and make him part of their pet-sitting team.

7 What change should be made in sentence 17?

  A. change *mine* to **myself**

  B. change *love* to **loves**

  C. delete the comma after *fiction*

  D. delete the word *a*

Read the introduction and the passage "An Awe-Inspiring Field Trip" before answering Numbers 8 through 14.

Steven wrote this passage about a field trip to a museum. Read his passage and think about the changes he should make.

An Awe-Inspiring Field Trip

(1) Our class field trip to the Regional Museum of Culture was a big surprise to me. (2) I expected the exhibit about ancient Egypt to be a little boring, but I was wrong. (3) It was one of the most fascinating things I have ever see!

(4) It didn't take long to figure out that this exhibit was something special. (5) As soon as we walked into the first room, we all gasped. (6) The room was darkened except for little spotlights on shimmering artifacts spread around the room. (7) The shimmering turned out to be the lights reflecting on gold! (8) There were golden statues, earrings,

bracelets, breastplates, and more. (9) The most breathtaking artifact which

is over 2,000 years old, was a mask from a mummy. (10) The mask looked

like the face of a real person, except for its brillint golden skin!

(11) In the next room were more artifacts that had been buried with

royalty and other powerful Egyptians. (12) Many objects were decorated

with gems, delicate carvings, or painted designs. (13) These objects

showed the wealth the person with whom they were buried.

(14) Other artifacts from the tombs were personal items that the person

enjoyed in life. (15) There were hair combs, wigs, and make-up that both

men and women used. (16) A pair of sandals in the exhibit weren't much

different from the ones I like to wear in the summer. (17) They were

wove from plant fiber and still looked almost new! (18) There was even a

wooden board game that egyptian children used to play.

(19) Those everyday items were what interested me most. (20) I

could easily imagine Ancient Egyptians holding them and using them.

(21) It was awe-inspiring to be so close to things that were thousands

of years old. (22) It made me understand why historians can get excited

about the past. (23) History became my favorite subject!

Now answer Numbers 8 through 14 on your Answer Sheet. Base your answers on the changes Steven should make.

8 What change should be made in sentence 3?

    F. change *one* to **won**

    G. change *most* to **more**

    H. change *see* to **seen**

    I. change the exclamation point to a question mark

9 What change should be made in sentence 9?

    A. change *most* to **more**

    B. insert a comma after *artifact*

    C. change *is* to **are**

    D. change *years* to **year**

10 What change should be made in sentence 10?

    F. change *real* to **reel**

    G. change *except* to **accept**

    H. change *its* to **it's**

    I. change *brillint* to **brilliant**

11 What change should be made in sentence 13?

    A. change *These* to **This**

    B. change *objects* to **object**

    C. change *showed* to **showing**

    D. insert **of** after *wealth*

12 What change should be made in sentence 17?

F. change *wove* to **woven**

G. insert a comma after *and*

H. change *looked* to **looks**

I. change *almost* to **allmost**

13 What change should be made in sentence 18?

A. change *There* to **They're**

B. change *board* to **bored**

C. change *egyptian* to **Egyptian**

D. change *used* to **use**

14 What is the best way to revise sentence 23?

F. Until then, history became my favorite subject!

G. On the other hand, history became my favorite subject!

H. Do you know that history became my favorite subject?

I. As a result of that field trip, history became my favorite subject!

Read the introduction and the passage "A Friend to the Rescue" before answering Numbers 15 through 20.

Laura wrote this passage about how a friend helped her at a track meet. Read her passage and think about the changes she should make.

A Friend to the Rescue

(1) I'll never forget the day that Marisa and I became friends.

(2) She turned what could have been a dreadful day into a great one.

(3) It all happened at our annual track-and-field meet. (4) I am passionate about running and I was signed up for two events the four-hundred-yard dash and a relay in which four team members each run one hundred yards. (5) Everyone on my relay team was a passionate runner, and we each had high hopes of winning until the week before the event. (6) Our teammate Lisa injured a muscle in one of her calfs and had to drop out of the race. (7) Who would take their place with the competition just days away?

(8) We soon found out. (9) During our training sessions, Marisa gave her best effort and showed herself to be a tough competitor, though she wasn't as fast as Lisa had been.

(10) On the day of the meet I lined up for the four-hundred-yard dash and noticed that Marisa was competing, too. (11) I didn't think I'd have any difficulty outrunning her. (12) However, as we passed the halfway mark, I was astonished to see that Marisa had taken the lead. (13) I tried to pull ahead, but I stumbled and fell. (14) From the opposite side of the track, Marisa saw me sprawled on the ground. (15) While the other

Name _____ Date _____

runners sprinted toward the finish, Marisa stepped off the track and ran

over to help me. (16) She was moments away from winning race, and she

sacrificed the blue ribbon to make sure I was okay.

(17) As Marisa helped me limp to the bleachers, the spectators

cheered. (18) Our teammates were disappointed at the loss, but they

understood what Marisa did. (19) Even though I hurt myself and didn't

win any races at that meet, I consider it my lucky day. (20) Marisa has

been my best friend ever since.

_____

Now answer Numbers 15 through 20 on your Answer Sheet. Base your answers on the changes Laura should make.

15 What change should be made in sentence 5?

   A. change *was* to **have**

   B. change *passionate* to **passionful**

   C. insert the word **who** after *each*

   D. insert a dash after *winning*

16 What change should be made in sentence 6?

   F. change *injured* to **injures**

   G. change *her* to **hers**

   H. change *calfs* to **calves**

   I. change *had* to **has**

17 What change should be made in sentence 7?

    A. change *Who* to **What**

    B. change *would* to **will**

    C. change *their* to **her**

    D. change *just* to **in**

18 Which sentence could best be added after sentence 8?

    F. There was no chance of Lisa recovering in time for the meet.

    G. With only days left to practice, we had to work harder than ever.

    H. The coach assigned a new student named Marisa to take Lisa's place.

    I. For weeks, we had been cooperating and improving our performance.

19 What change should be made in sentence 10?

    A. insert a comma after *meet*

    B. change *noticed* to **notice**

    C. change *competing* to **competed**

    D. change *too* to **to**

20 What change should be made in sentence 16?

    F. change *moments* to **momentarily**

    G. insert **that** after *winning*

    H. insert a comma after *ribbon*

    I. change the period to a question mark

Name _____ Date _____

Writing to Inform

Read the prompt and plan your response.

Most places offer a variety of community events that are fun.

Think about an event in your community that is fun.

Now write to inform readers about the event in your community and why you think it is fun.

Planning Page

Use this space to make your notes before you begin writing. The writing on this page will NOT be scored.

_____

_____

_____

_____

_____

_____

_____

_____

_____

_____

_____

_____

_____

Begin writing your response here. The writing on this page and the next page
WILL be scored.

_____

_____

_____

_____

_____

_____

_____

_____

_____

_____

_____

_____

_____

_____

_____

_____

_____

_____

_____

_____

_____

_____

_____

_____

_____

_____

_____

_____

_____

_____

_____

_____

_____

_____

_____

_____

_____

_____

_____

_____

_____

_____

_____

_____

_____

_____

_____

_____

_____

Reading Complex Text

Read the passage "The Story of Prometheus: How Fire Was Given to Men." As you read, stop and answer each question. Use evidence from the passage to support your answers.

The Story of Prometheus: How Fire Was Given to Men

from *Old Greek Stories* by James Baldwin

Prometheus did not care to live amid the clouds on the mountaintop. He was too busy for that. While the Mighty Folk were spending their time in idleness, drinking nectar and eating ambrosia, he was intent upon plans for making the world wiser and better than it had ever been before.

He went out amongst men to live with them and help them; for his heart was filled with sadness when he found that they were no longer happy as they had been during the golden days when Saturn was king. Ah, how very poor and wretched they were! He found them living in caves and in holes of the earth, shivering with the cold because there was no fire, dying of starvation, hunted by wild beasts and by one another – the most miserable of all living creatures.

"If they only had fire," said Prometheus to himself, "they could at least warm themselves and cook their food; and after a while they could learn to make tools and build themselves houses. Without fire, they are worse off than the beasts."

1 How does Prometheus set himself apart from the other Mighty Folk?

_____

_____

_____

Then he went boldly to Jupiter and begged him to give fire to men, so that they might have a little comfort through the long, dreary months of winter.

"Not a spark will I give," said Jupiter. "No, indeed! Why, if men had fire they might become strong and wise like ourselves, and after a while they would drive us out of our kingdom. Let them shiver with cold, and let them live like the

Name _____ Date _____

beasts. It is best for them to be poor and ignorant, that so we Mighty Ones may thrive and be happy."

Prometheus made no answer; but he had set his heart on helping mankind, and he did not give up. He turned away, and left Jupiter and his mighty company forever.

---

2 What happens as a result of Jupiter's refusal to give fire to mankind?

_____

_____

_____

As he was walking by the shore of the sea he found a reed, or, as some say, a tall stalk of fennel, growing; and when he had broken it off he saw that its hollow center was filled with a dry, soft pith which would burn slowly and keep on fire a long time. He took the long stalk in his hands, and started with it towards the dwelling of the sun in the far east.

"Mankind shall have fire in spite of the tyrant who sits on the mountaintop," he said.

He reached the place of the sun in the early morning just as the glowing, golden orb rose from the earth and began its daily journey through the sky. He touched the end of the long reed to the flames, and the dry pith caught on fire and burned slowly. Then he turned and hastened back to his own land, carrying with him the precious spark hidden in the hollow center of the plant.

---

3 How does the scene above contribute to the plot's development?

_____

_____

_____

He called some of the shivering men from their caves and built a fire for them, and showed them how to warm themselves by it and how to build other fires from the coals. Soon there was a cheerful blaze in every rude home in the land, and men and women gathered round it and were warm and happy, and thankful to Prometheus for the wonderful gift which he had brought to them from the sun.

152

Name _____ Date _____

4 Describe Prometheus's attitude toward mankind. How does the author use this attitude to help convey the central idea of the passage?

_____

_____

_____

_____

_____

Reading and Analyzing Text

Read the article "Who Turned on the Faucet?" before answering Numbers 1 through 6.

Who Turned on the Faucet?

by Sarah E. Romanov
illustrated by Brian Biggs

You walk into the kitchen while someone is chopping onions. A cold wind hits you in the face when you turn a corner on the street. You fall off your bike and scrape your knee. You watch a sad movie with your friends. What do all of these things have in common? They can all turn on the faucets in your eyes, sending rivers of warm tears flowing down your cheeks! Your tears might embarrass you at times, but they're very important to your eyes.

Tear glands under your upper eyelids are responsible for making tears, which are made of water, proteins, hormones[1], and a special oil that helps protect your eyes. If you've ever tasted your tears, you know they're also salty.

As tears wash down over your eyeballs, they drain out through tear ducts—tiny tubes that run between your eyes and nose. Look in a mirror and pull down your lower eyelid a bit. Do you see a little hole in the corner near your nose? That's the opening of a tear duct. If your eyes are watering, those tear ducts keep the flow under control. But if you start to cry, the ducts can't drain the tears quickly enough so they overflow, running down your face. Because tear ducts connect your eyes and nose, when your eyes water and your nose gets runny, you grab a tissue and blow out . . . tears! That's right, those are tears that have drained from your eyes into your nose.

Shedding tears is your body's way of giving your eyes the protection and moisture they need. In fact, you constantly make just enough tears to make sure your eyes aren't too dry. Blinking coats the eyes with this special moisturizer, called continuous tears, all day long.

Other tears called reflex tears flow to protect your eyes from things that aren't supposed to be in them. That is why you get teary-eyed when it's windy. Your eyes

[1] **hormones:** chemical substances produced in the body that control and regulate the activity of certain cells or organs

Name _____ Date _____

know that wind can dry them out fast, so they do their best to keep things wet! And when a piece of sand or an eyelash gets into your eye, those faucets turn on full-force to wash the invader out. So why does just the smell of onions make your eyes water? It's not really the smell—when an onion is cut, it releases chemicals that irritate your eyes.

Emotional tears are the least understood kind of tears. They flow when you watch a sad movie, get angry with someone, are very afraid, or even receive exciting news that makes you happy. Sometimes just seeing someone crying can make you cry, even if you don't feel sad yourself. Some people cry easily, while others have a hard time shedding tears.

Among others, Dr. William Frey, a scientist from Minnesota, has spent many years studying tears. When Dr. Frey needed samples of tears to study, volunteers watched sad movies and collected their tears in little bottles for him. He discovered that emotional

tears contain larger amounts of certain chemicals and hormones than the other types of tears do. Your body produces these substances in response to stress.

When people are very stressed and have too many of these hormones and chemicals in their bodies, they can become sick, both physically and emotionally. Dr. Frey believes that shedding emotional tears releases these bad substances and helps maintain your body's proper chemical balance. This might explain why you feel better after a good cry.

There are still many mysteries about tears and crying that future research might explain. Scientists like Dr. Frey are working very hard to solve these mysteries. In the meantime, whenever you blink your eyes, smell freshly cut onions, or watch a sad movie, grab a tissue and be thankful for the wonderful way tears help take care of your body!

Now answer Numbers 1 through 6 on your Answer Sheet. Base your answers on the article "Who Turned on the Faucet?"

1 Why does the author introduce the article by giving examples of times when people cry?

    A. to establish a serious tone for the article

    B. to appeal to readers' own experiences crying

    C. to give readers background on how tears are produced

    D. to convince readers that they should not be embarrassed about crying

2 Read this excerpt from the article.

> **What do all of these things have in common? They can all turn on the faucets in your eyes, sending rivers of warm tears flowing down your cheeks!**

Why does the author use the phrase *they can all turn on the faucets* in the sentence above?

    F. to imply that tear ducts can leak even when we are not crying

    G. to show that it is difficult for people to stop crying once they start

    H. to demonstrate the great speed and volume at which our tears can flow

    I. to express that we don't always have control over when we produce tears

3 The three kinds of tears described in this article are

    A. protein, hormone, and oil.

    B. balance, invasion, and stress.

    C. continuous, reflex, and emotional.

    D. protective, moisturizing, and reactive.

Name _____ Date _____

4 As used in the article, which pair of words is most similar in meaning?

   F. explain, solve

   G. protection, control

   H. samples, volunteers

   I. responsible, thankful

5 A reader could validly conclude from the article that

   A. all tears are the same.

   B. all animals shed tears.

   C. some people never shed tears.

   D. tears are a part of good health.

6 How did Dr. Frey conduct his scientific research?

   F. He read about tears.

   G. He chopped many onions.

   H. He studied stress in people.

   I. He asked volunteers to watch sad movies.

Name _____ Date _____

Read the passage "Friends Forever" and the excerpt from *My Ántonia* **before answering Numbers 7 through 13.**

Friends Forever

June 15

Dear Chris,

Hello at long last from the Big Apple. I can't quite comprehend that I've been in New York this long without writing to you. I'm still not thrilled that we had to relocate here. For the first two whole weeks, nothing was unpacked, so it was like we were camping out in our own apartment. It took such a long time because our new apartment is so much smaller than our old house in San Francisco.

After unpacking, we spent a couple of weeks exploring our new neighborhood, which is really different from the one in San Francisco. Our apartment is in what's referred to as the East Village of Manhattan. There are no skyscrapers around here, just ancient brick apartment buildings, mostly four or five stories tall, with lots of little stores and interesting restaurants. Three blocks to the north is a park with a skatepark that I can't wait to try out, and right next to that is my future middle school, so I won't have to take a bus. It's strange because it looks similar to our old school—all brick and concrete with teeny tiny windows. I'm looking forward to showing you around.

Your friend,

Arnie

June 25

Dear Chris,

I've spent several days at the Metropolitan Museum, which is another reason why I haven't been able to write to you. The museum was the primary reason we had to move out here—it's where my mom works now. The building is absolutely enormous. There are so many exhibits to explore that I still haven't seen a quarter of them, and I've been there three times!

Once, while Mom was still working at the museum, Dad and I took an elevator to the observation deck of the Empire State Building. When we looked out, all we saw was a brick wall of fog. Dad and I just stared at each other and laughed! Clearly, it's not only San Francisco that is famous for fog.

Another time, Dad and I ventured to see the barge and tanker traffic on the Hudson River. Later that same day, we met Mom in Central Park and went to see a Shakespearean play called *Julius Caesar* in an amphitheater[1] there. So you can see, there's a lot to do around here.

Your friend,

Arnie

July 8

Dear Chris,

I'm now in my bedroom, which is so cramped and tiny that my bed and desk occupy almost all the floor space, leaving hardly any room to stretch out on the carpet the way I like to. My bed is next to a window, which looks out on the air conditioning vent that runs through the building, and when I lie down and concentrate, I can hear all sorts of interesting noises coming through the vents. Right now there's a lady singing the same opera song over and over. Last night, I heard chanting. There are several families from foreign countries that live in my building. I think I have heard at least three languages, not including English.

Did I tell you that our building has its own doorman? Well, it does, and the doorman's son, Harvey, invited me to his house in Brooklyn. He's pretty normal, except that he's been studying karate since he was a toddler and goes to competitions with his dad in Japan! His dad has a twelfth degree black belt, and he teaches at the *dojo*, which is why Harvey's been practicing karate since he was two. The great news is that I'm going to their martial arts school starting next week.

[1] **amphitheater:** a round or oval building with tiers of seats around a central, open area

We went up on the roof of our building the evening of the Fourth of July and had a perfect view of the fireworks, which they shoot off from a barge in the East River. Everyone in the building was up there with their friends, and people were barbecuing. It was really weird to watch from the top of the building instead of at a park, but I think I could get used to it. The fireworks display was intense and the barbecue was delicious.

I can't wait until you arrive—four weeks seems like forever. There are so many interesting places that I want to introduce you to, and you'll have to meet Harvey and the three brothers who live just down the hall. We'll definitely all have to go to the skatepark.

Your friend,

Arnie

An excerpt from *My Ántonia*

by Willa Cather

. . . I was ten years old then; I had lost both my father and mother within a year, and my Virginia relatives were sending me out to my grandparents, who lived in Nebraska. I travelled in the care of a mountain boy, Jake Marpole, one of the "hands" on my father's old farm under the Blue Ridge, who was now going West to work for my grandfather. Jake's experience of the world was not much wider than mine. He had never been in a railway train until the morning when we set out together to try our fortunes in a new world.

We went all the way in day-coaches, becoming more sticky and grimy with each stage of the journey. Jake bought everything the newsboys offered him: candy, oranges, brass collar buttons, a watch-charm, and for me a *Life of Jesse James*, which I remember as one of the most satisfactory books I have ever read. Beyond Chicago we were under the protection of a friendly passenger conductor, who knew all about the country to which we were going and gave us a great deal of advice in exchange for our confidence. He seemed to us an experienced and worldly man who had been almost everywhere; in his conversation he threw out lightly the names of distant states and cities…

Once when he sat down to chat, he told us that in the immigrant car ahead there was a family from "across the water" whose destination was the same as ours.

"They can't any of them speak English, except one little girl, and all she can say is 'We go Black Hawk, Nebraska.' She's not much older than you, twelve or thirteen, maybe, and she's as bright as a new dollar. Don't you want to go ahead and see her, Jimmy? She's got the pretty brown eyes, too!"

This last remark made me bashful, and I shook my head and settled down to 'Jesse James'…

I do not remember crossing the Missouri River, or anything about the long day's journey through Nebraska. Probably by that time I had crossed so many rivers that I was dull to them. The only thing very noticeable about Nebraska was that it was still, all day long, Nebraska.

I had been sleeping, curled up in a red plush seat, for a long while when we reached Black Hawk. Jake roused me and took me by the hand. We stumbled down from the train to a wooden siding, where men were running about with lanterns. I couldn't see any town, or even distant lights; we were surrounded by utter darkness. The engine was panting heavily after its long run. In the red glow from the fire-box, a group of people stood huddled together on the platform, encumbered by bundles and boxes. I knew this must be the immigrant family the conductor had told us about. The woman wore a fringed shawl tied over her head, and she carried a little tin trunk in her arms, hugging it as if it were a baby. There

Name _____ Date _____

was an old man, tall and stooped. Two half-grown boys and a girl stood holding oilcloth bundles, and a little girl clung to her mother's skirts. Presently a man with a lantern approached them and began to talk, shouting and exclaiming. I pricked up my ears, for it was positively the first time I had ever heard a foreign tongue[1].

Another lantern came along. A bantering voice called out: "Hello, are you Mr. Burden's folks? If you are, it's me you're looking for. I'm Otto Fuchs. I'm Mr. Burden's hired man, and I'm to drive you out. Hello, Jimmy, ain't you scared to come so far west?"

I looked up with interest at the new face in the lantern-light. He might have stepped out of the pages of *Jesse James*. He wore a sombrero hat, with a wide leather band and a bright buckle, and the ends of his moustache were twisted up stiffly, like little horns. He looked lively and ferocious, I thought, and as if he had a history. A long scar ran across one cheek and drew the corner of his mouth up in a sinister curl. . . . As he walked about the platform in his high-heeled boots, looking for our trunks, I saw that he was a rather slight man, quick and wiry, and light on his feet. He told us we had a long night drive ahead of us, and had better be on the hike. He led us to a hitching-bar where two farm-wagons were tied, and I saw the foreign family crowding into one of them. The other was for us. Jake got on the front seat with Otto Fuchs, and I rode on the straw in the bottom of the wagon-box, covered up with a buffalo hide. The immigrants rumbled off into the empty darkness, and we followed them.

I tried to go to sleep, but the jolting made me bite my tongue, and I soon began to ache all over. When the straw settled down, I had a hard bed. Cautiously I slipped from under the buffalo hide, got up on my knees and peered over the side of the wagon. There seemed to be nothing to see; no fences, no creeks or trees, no hills or fields. If there was a road, I could not make it out in the faint starlight. There was nothing but land: not a country at all, but the material out of which countries are made. No, there was nothing but land—slightly undulating[2], I knew, because often our wheels ground against the brake as we went down into a hollow and lurched up again on the other side. I had the feeling that the world was left behind, that we had got over the edge of it, and were outside man's jurisdiction. I had never before looked up at the sky when there was not a familiar mountain ridge against it...

[1] **tongue:** language

[2] **undulating:** moving in a wavelike motion

Now answer Numbers 7 through 13 on your Answer Sheet. Base your answers on the passage "Friends Forever" and the excerpt from *My Ántonia.*

7 Read this sentence from the passage "Friends Forever."

> **When we looked out, all we saw was a brick wall of fog.**

Why does the author use the phrase *a brick wall of fog* in the sentence above?

A. to highlight the fog's dark color.

B. to emphasize the fog's thickness.

C. to show how cold the fog makes the air feel.

D. to imply that Arnie wasn't expecting to see fog in New York.

8 Based on the last letter, dated July 8, the reader can tell that Arnie

F. no longer misses Chris and his life in San Francisco.

G. is beginning to adapt, and even enjoy, life in New York.

H. is having a difficult time adjusting to living in New York.

I. is reluctant to have Chris meet his new friends in New York.

9 Which words from the excerpt from *My Ántonia* are most OPPOSITE in meaning?

A. satisfactory, lively

B. friendly, ferocious

C. experienced, worldly

D. exclaiming, bantering

10 Read this excerpt from *My Ántonia*.

> Jake roused me and took me by the hand. We stumbled down from the train to a wooden siding, where men were running about with lanterns. I couldn't see any town, or even distant lights; we were surrounded by utter darkness.

Which of the following words best describes the scene above?

F. confused

G. hopeful

H. pleasant

I. welcoming

11 How does the last paragraph of the excerpt from *My Ántonia* contribute to the development of the setting?

A. It shows how desolate and unfamiliar the Nebraska landscape is to the narrator.

B. It focuses on the worn, bumpy path, which shows how well-traveled Nebraska is.

C. It shows how populated Nebraska is compared to where the narrator is coming from.

D. It emphasizes the beauty of the Nebraska landscape and its unique, varied vegetation.

12 Both the passage "Friends Forever" and the excerpt from *My Ántonia* deal with themes of

F. friendship and love.

G. compromise and sacrifice.

H. change and new experiences.

I. overcoming ambition and pride.

13 How do the experiences of Arnie in "Friends Forever" and the narrator, Jimmy, in the excerpt from *My Ántonia* differ at the end of each passage?

A. Arnie still feels lonely in New York, while Jimmy is surrounded by loving relatives.

B. Arnie decides that he prefers his new life, while Jimmy cannot get used to life in Nebraska.

C. Arnie desperately wants to return to San Francisco, while Jimmy is content to be in Nebraska.

D. Arnie has begun to settle into his new apartment, while Jimmy has not yet arrived at his new home.

Read the passage "Watch Out!" before answering Numbers 14 through 19.

Watch Out!

as told by Joe Hayes
illustrated by Vicki Trego Hill

Once a poor couple struggled together to make a living from a tiny farm. They were hard-working people, but their farm was so small and the soil was so poor that they were never able to get ahead. Each winter they ended up eating the seed for the next year's crop, and each spring they had to go to the money-lender in the village and borrow money to buy seeds so that they could plant again.

And then all year long they had to worry whether they would make enough to pay back the debt. Some years they were forced to be late in their payments, and then the money-lender would torment them with threats to take their small farm away from them.

Finally the year they had dreaded for so long arrived. Between hail in June and grasshoppers in August, hardly enough remained of their crop at harvest time to keep them alive through the winter. There was nothing left over to sell for cash to pay back the money-lender.

The poor couple didn't know what to do. Each time they went to the village, they carefully avoided the money-lender's house for fear that he would rush out and demand payment of them. Each day they watched the road in front of their farm nervously, sure that this was the day the money-lender would arrive to take their land away from them.

And then one Sunday, as they were leaving the village church and starting for home, the couple met up face to face with the money-lender in the center of the village plaza. Just as they had expected, the money-lender immediately demanded payment. "My money is long overdue," he told them. "If you don't pay me this very day, tomorrow I will take possession of your farm."

The poor people pleaded with the money-lender. "Please," they said, "take pity on us. It has been a very bad year, as you know. Next year we'll pay you double."

"Take pity?" the money-lender said scornfully. "Haven't I overlooked your late payments year after year? But now you've gone too far. I must have my money immediately, or your farm is mine."

Of course, the plaza was crowded with people leaving the church, and they soon began to notice the discussion between the couple and the money-lender. They gathered around to listen.

The money-lender noticed the crowd around them and began to grow uncomfortable. He didn't want to appear too hard-hearted. If he did, people might be too frightened to borrow money from him in the future.

"Very well," the money-lender told the farmer, "Let it never be said that I am unwilling to give people every possible opportunity. And besides, I'm in a playful mood this morning. I'll give you a chance to be free from your debt. Do you see how the ground here in the plaza is covered with pebbles, some white, some black? I will pick up one pebble of each color and hold them in my closed fist. You may reach a finger in and pull out one pebble. If the pebble is black, your debt will be forgiven. You will owe me nothing. If the pebble you choose is white, your farm is mine this day."

The poor farmer had no choice but to agree, although he didn't really trust the money-lender to keep his word. The farmer and his wife watched as the money-lender knelt down and picked up two pebbles from the ground. No one else caught it, but the husband and wife saw that the money-lender had actually picked up two white pebbles. But they couldn't say anything because they knew the money-lender would just pretend to be insulted and throw the pebbles back into the ground and withdraw his offer.

"Are you ready?" asked the money-lender, with a sly smile on his face. He held out his hand with the fingers closed tightly over the two pebbles.

Filled with despair, the farmer reached toward the money-lender's hands, but his wife stopped him. "Wait!" she told him. "Let me choose. This feels like my lucky day."

The farmer quickly agreed, and the woman closed her eyes as if she were concentrating deeply. She took several deep breaths, and then reached out slowly toward the money-lender's closed fist. She seemed to be trembling with

Name _____ Date _____

nervousness. She pried the fingers open and withdrew one pebble. And then she seemed to tremble even more violently. And she dropped the pebble! A gasp went up from the crowd.

"Oh, no!" cried the woman. "How clumsy of me!" But then she said to the money-lender, "Oh, well. It doesn't matter. There were only two colors of pebbles. Show us which color is left in your hand. The one I dropped had to be the other color."

"You're right," said everyone in the crowd, and they all told the money-lender, "Show us which color is left."

Grudgingly the money-lender opened his fist. "It's white!" everyone cried. "The one the woman chose had to be black." And they all began to congratulate the couple.

The money-lender forced a smile and shook the farmer's hand. "Congratulations," he said. And to the woman he added, "So this really was your lucky day. But take my advice, both of you. In the future, watch out that you don't get yourselves into such a position again."

"We will," said the farmer, smiling broadly. "And you, sir, in the future, watch out for clever women!"

The people in the crowd didn't quite know what the farmer was referring to, but the money-lender knew exactly what he meant, and he walked away grumbling to himself.

Now answer Numbers 14 through 19 on your Answer Sheet. Base your answers on the passage "Watch Out!"

14 Read this sentence from the passage.

> **Some years they were forced to be late in their payments, and then the money-lender would torment them with threats to take their small farm away from them.**

What word or words in the sentence above help readers understand the meaning of the word *torment*?

F. some years

G. payments

H. threats

I. small farm

15 The money-lender offers the poor couple a chance to wipe out their debt to

A. pay off his own debt.

B. protect the future of his business.

C. get double his payment from them.

D. persuade the woman to work for him.

16 Read this sentence from the passage.

> **He didn't want to appear too hard-hearted.**

Why does the phrase *hard-hearted* mean in the sentence above?

F. irritable

G. passive

H. picky

I. unfeeling

17 Read this sentence from the passage.

> **The farmer quickly agreed, and the woman closed her eyes as if she were concentrating deeply.**

What does the word *concentrating* mean in the sentence above?

A. approving

B. forgetting

C. sleeping

D. thinking

18 What causes the woman to drop the pebble?

F. She is scared that she has selected the wrong pebble.

G. She is concentrating so deeply that she accidentally lets go of the pebble.

H. She is so confident that it is her lucky day that her actions become careless.

I. She knows the money-lender cheated and tries to trick him at his own game.

Name _____ Date _____

19 How does the point of view of the narrator contribute to the reader's understanding of the passage?

A. It forces readers to infer all of the characters' thoughts and feelings.

B. It enables readers to access only the poor woman's inner thoughts and feelings.

C. It allows readers to experience the action in the passage as if they are people in the village.

D. It gives readers access to the inner thoughts and feelings of the poor couple and the money-lender.

Read the article "Public Libraries" before answering Numbers 20 through 24.

Public Libraries

Many towns across the United States have public libraries, places where people can borrow books, movies, or CDs. Children can listen to stories or participate in summer reading programs, and adults can take computer classes or take part in book discussions. These libraries are called public for several reasons. First, these services are provided for the public. Second, the services provided by the libraries cost money, which comes from the public. Third, libraries grew out of the actions of ordinary people who saw that there was a need to educate people and came together to find a way to meet that need.

One of the earlier libraries in the United States was started by Benjamin Franklin. In the early days of the nation, books were expensive and hard to find, so Franklin decided to form a group of people who would pool their money to purchase books. He created a subscription library. These subscription libraries started appearing throughout the country but were available only to members who paid a yearly fee, or subscription, for the right to borrow books.

In the mid-1800s, women formed literary societies, or reading groups. At that time, women did not get the same education as men; in order to educate themselves, and each other, they formed groups. The literary societies they formed would share and discuss books to increase their knowledge about the world.

As these societies grew, women realized the education gained from books should be accessible to everyone, not just those who could afford the yearly subscription fee. They started to create their own libraries. These libraries started as library associations, whose missions were to make books accessible. Library associations accomplished that by taking over existing subscription libraries, raising money to buy books, and collecting donations of book collections from citizens. Though these libraries started small, their collections grew and they became popular. It wasn't necessary to purchase a subscription for these libraries, so more and more people were able to access the books in the collections.

As these libraries grew, two new problems arose and the societies turned to the public to help solve them. First, the collections grew too big to fit in existing buildings. As a result, some associations raised money from the community to purchase new buildings. In other communities, buildings that could serve as libraries were donated by wealthy citizens. Second, the societies could not raise enough money to cover the cost of running the libraries. They realized that the government could help with those costs. By 1900, most libraries were supported by the public with tax money.

Libraries grew out of the idea that people should have a chance to better themselves through education. Giving the public access to books through libraries was one way to address this goal. When the public took over running libraries, through their tax dollars, libraries truly became public in all senses of the word. Many libraries still in existence today in the United States owe their start to a small group of local people who planted the seed of the wonderful library that the public continues to enjoy.

1638—The oldest library in the United States was founded, becoming the Harvard University Library.

1731—A subscription library association, The Library Company of Philadelphia, was founded by Benjamin Franklin.

1849—The New York Public Library started.

1854—Boston Public Library opened to the public on March 20. It was the first to be supported by direct public taxation.

Now answer Numbers 20 through 24 on your Answer Sheet. Base your answers on the article "Public Libraries."

20 Which of the following best tells how the author introduces the concept of public libraries in the article?

   F. by posing questions to readers about public libraries in their towns

   G. by explaining several reasons why public libraries are called "public"

   H. by describing the idea Benjamin Franklin first had for public libraries

   I. by relaying an anecdote of someone's experience using a public library

21 Read this sentence from the article.

> **Library associations accomplished that by taking over existing
> subscription libraries, raising money to buy books, and collecting
> donations of book collections from citizens.**

The word *donations* comes from the Latin root meaning

A. call.

B. give.

C. grow.

D. move.

22 Which of the following best describes how the text structure of the second-to-last
paragraph, which begins, "As these libraries grew, . . ." contributes to the development
of the author's central idea?

F. The author uses cause-and-effect to show why women began to create their
own library associations.

G. The author uses problem-solution to show how the public helped solve
problems facing library associations.

H. The author uses a sequence of events to help readers understand how the
country's earliest libraries developed.

I. The author uses comparison-contrast to help readers distinguish between
library associations and subscription libraries.

23 What can readers tell from both the information in the article and in the timeline?

A. why Benjamin Franklin invented a library

B. why public libraries were started in New England

C. the history of public libraries over two hundred years

D. how public libraries were started by women in small communities

24 Based on the article, what judgment can the reader make about public libraries?

F. They serve children more than adults.

G. They are an example of community action.

H. They are quiet places where one can study.

I. They hold more books than school libraries.

Read the article "Limber Wood and Shallow Roots" before answering Numbers 25 through 30.

Limber Wood and Shallow Roots

It was April, and the wind howled like a hungry coyote as a storm approached. Jasper's Uncle Ken, his mother's brother, was visiting to install new brakes on the family car. "Wind's coming up," Ken mumbled as he came into the house, chewing a toothpick and wiping his hands on an oil-stained bandana.

The door slammed violently behind him, and Ken and his sister exchanged knowing glances. Rain pelted the windows and the roof, sounding like horses running wild, while the wind howled as though it would like to tear the house apart. Jasper's mother threw sand into the stove, extinguishing the fire, and the three of them walked outside to take shelter in the root cellar. Clinging to each other to avoid being blown away by the persistent wind, they fought to walk the handful of steps from the door to the cellar. Ken entered into a wrestling match with the door, but he finally managed to wrench it open. Jasper and his mother scrambled quickly inside.

Once inside, Jasper and Ken crouched in a corner, while Jasper's mother found the blankets that they kept in the cellar along with water and food in case of emergencies like this. She also found the small battery-powered radio. Turning it on, she learned that the winds had reached over seventy-five miles per hour. After that, the radio kept replaying the high-pitched tone indicating that there was an emergency. The announcer said where tornadoes had been sighted and where they had touched down.

Suddenly, over the radio signal, they heard a new sound: a rhythmic creaking followed by a long, low moan, like a bellowing cow. Seconds later, the first tree hit the roof, toppling the chimney. They could smell the soot from the inside of the chimney, and Jasper's mother reached for him.

As they sat huddled in the cellar waiting out the storm, they heard at least a dozen more trees give in to the wind. They heard the roots let go with that same eerie groan, and then the pines hit the roof—almost gently—since their bendable trunks didn't break and their shallow roots let them easily pull away from the earth. Finally, an hour after it began, the storm lessened, the trees stopped creaking, and the radio started playing music again and relaying optimistic news.

They emerged from the cellar to blue skies with fluffy white clouds and clean-washed air. Branches were everywhere and half a dozen trees leaned on the roof, but miraculously no windows had been broken. Jasper and his mother just stood there, gaping at the way the trees almost seemed to caress the outside walls of the house. "Wow," Jasper finally whispered as they stepped over trunks and branches. "We were lucky, weren't we?"

"We *are* lucky," his mother replied. "All that's broken is the chimney, and that can be repaired easily. We're lucky those trees are pines—limber wood and shallow roots probably saved our windows and our roof."

Now answer Numbers 25 through 30 on your Answer Sheet. Base your answers on the passage "Limber Wood and Shallow Roots."

25 What is the main conflict that the family in the passage faces?

A. A violent storm forces them to leave their house and seek shelter in the cellar.

B. They resist going to the cellar because they don't believe the storm will get worse.

C. The storm damages dozens of trees in their yard, as well as the walls of their house.

D. When they finally decide to seek shelter from the storm, they cannot open the cellar door.

26 The writer compares the rain to

F. horses running wild.

G. a tornado touching down.

H. a hungry howling animal.

I. limber wood and shallow roots.

Name _____ Date _____

27 Read this sentence from the passage.

> Ken entered into a wrestling match with the door, but he finally managed to wrench it open.

Why does the writer compare the door to a person engaged in a wrestling match with Ken?

A. to show how Ken struggled to open the door

B. to show how worried Ken is about the storm

C. to suggest that the door is very old and nearly rotten

D. to imply that the cellar hasn't been used in a long time

28 By listening to the radio, the characters learn

F. that their house survived the storm.

G. that tornadoes have been sighted nearby.

H. that they need to seek shelter in the cellar.

I. why pine trees cause less damage than other trees.

29 Read this sentence from the passage.

> They heard the roots let go with that same eerie groan, and then the pines hit the roof—almost gently—since their bendable trunks didn't break and their shallow roots let them easily pull away from the earth.

What does the word *bendable* mean in the sentence above?

A. dense

B. durable

C. flexible

D. narrow

30 Which word from the passage has a positive connotation?

F. approached

G. caress

H. huddled

I. smell

Read the article "EMU" before answering Numbers 31 through 35.

EMU

An EMU is an Extravehicular Mobility Unit, a special kind of spacesuit used by astronauts while they are in space. *Extravehicular* means that they are used outside a space shuttle, a space station, or the vehicle. *Mobility* means that the suits let astronauts move around easily. They can even use their hands and fingers to perform fine motor tasks, such as repairing the space station. *Unit* means that although there are thousands of pieces and parts to these suits, they all function together to protect astronauts from space.

Space is a hostile place for human beings. In the dark, temperatures can reach 150 degrees below zero; in direct sunlight, the thermometer can hit 250 degrees. Both of these temperatures are more extreme than anything found on Earth. Space lacks air pressure and contains high levels of radiation[1]. Tiny meteoroids, old satellites, and even trash constantly zoom through the airless void.

An EMU does not depend on support from a space station or shuttle. Astronauts carry PLSS, or Portable Life Support Systems, on their backs. Because the systems provide oxygen, water, and temperature and air pressure control, astronauts who wear them can work outside for up to nine hours at a time.

EMUs are reusable. The pieces, which come from many standardized parts, can be fitted together in different ways to fit different astronauts. Somewhere, there is a huge closet of EMU parts: torsos and boots, gloves and helmets. The parts fit ninety percent of the population, and both men and women can wear them.

Astronauts do not wear the EMU inside the space station or shuttle. In order to go on a spacewalk, the astronauts must put the sections on in order.

1. Put on the underlayer. This is similar to long underwear but with tubes that help cool the suit.

2. Enter the airlock area, where the rest of the EMU will be put on.

3. Attach the communication equipment, life support system, and arms to the EMU.

4. Rub antifog goo onto the visor, so it remains clear.

5. Attach a mirror and checklist to the sleeves of the EMU. Place a food bar and drink bag inside for easy access.

6. Check the lights and cameras to make sure they work. Place the visor on the helmet. Connect the communications equipment. Check to make sure that the communications equipment works.

7. Step into the lower part of the EMU, which extends above the waist.

[1] **radiation:** streams of particles or electromagnetic waves given off by the atoms and molecules of a radioactive substance

8. Wiggle into the upper torso part. Attach the cooling tubes of the EMU into the life-support system. Attach the electricity to the life-support system.

9. Lock the lower part into the upper part of the EMU. Lock on the helmet.

10. Slip on the inner comfort gloves. Lock on the outer gloves.

After the EMU is on, the astronaut must check for leaks. If there are no leaks, the astronaut can leave the airlock[2] and enter space where, for the next nine hours, the EMU will be like the astronaut's own personal spacecraft. When the spacewalk is finished, all the steps are done, but in reverse. When completed, the astronaut can once again enter the shuttle or space station.

[2]**airlock:** an airtight chamber in which air pressure can be controlled

180

Name _____ Date _____

Now answer Numbers 31 through 35 on your Answer Sheet. Base your answers on the article "EMU."

31 Read this dictionary entry.

> **fine** (fahyn) *adjective*
>
> 1. excellent or admirable
>
> 2. very thin or slender
>
> 3. precise
>
> 4. being in a state of good health; quite well

Read this sentence from the article.

> **They can even use their hands and fingers to perform fine motor tasks, such as repairing the space station.**

Which meaning best fits the way the word *fine* is used in the sentence above?

A. meaning 1

B. meaning 2

C. meaning 3

D. meaning 4

32 Read this sentence from the article.

> **Space is a hostile place for human beings.**

What does the word *hostile* mean in the sentence above?

F. empty or deserted

G. unfavorable to health

H. causing fright or alarm

I. relating to the environment

33 Which details from the article support the need for EMUs?

    A. definitions of the initials

    B. facts about the harshness of space

    C. facts about who can wear an EMU

    D. explanations of various parts of an EMU

34 In the third paragraph, the author writes that the PLSS provides "oxygen, water, and temperature and air pressure control." The reader can conclude from this that

    F. the Portable Life Support Systems are not essential to astronauts.

    G. astronauts can work outside the space station for up to nine hours.

    H. astronauts in space need more oxygen and water than people on earth.

    I. humans need oxygen, water, and a certain temperature and air pressure to survive.

35 How does the use of sequence in the numbered list help the author develop the central idea in the article?

    A. It explains the various pieces of an EMU and their functions.

    B. It tells the steps an astronaut follows when putting on an EMU.

    C. It explains a set of tasks an astronaut accomplishes while wearing an EMU.

    D. It tells the steps an astronaut takes after leaving the airlock and entering space.

Revising and Editing

Read the introduction and the passage "A View from the Top" before answering Numbers 1 through 7.

Maria wrote this passage after visiting the Statue of Liberty. Read her passage and think about the changes she should make.

A View from the Top

(1) Standing 305 feet tall in New York Harbor, the Statue of Liberty is a majestic symbol of the United States. (2) Maybe you have seen pictures of the statue wearing a spiked crown and holding a torch. (3) During a Fourth of July celebration, I was honored to be one of 240 people who went inside the statue's crown. (4) We also visited an art museum that day.

(5) At ground level, ten people at a time entered into the base of the statue's pedestal. (6) Here I got to see the statue's original torch. (7) I got to photograph it. (8) The torch had been replaced long ago and then put on display. (9) Much taller than a person, the torch's enormity was absolutely shocking?

(10) Instead of taking an elevator to reach the top. (11) We had to climb 354 steps. (12) A spiral staircase of metal makes up the last 146 stairs. (13) Many of the steps are so narrow that the heel of my foot hung off the back, so I held tightly to the rail as a procaution. (14) It was a very much tiring climb.

(15) Once inside the crown, I was surprised at how small the space actually was. (16) Even though there were only ten people in the room, we had to stand side-by-side. (17) However, once I looked out one of the 25 windows, I quickly forgot the cramped space. (18) The breathtaking sight included the skylines of Brooklyn and Manhattan, bridges, and the setting sun reflecting off the water far below me.

(19) All too soon a park ranger told to begin the descent, it was time, but I won't soon forget my experience inside the crown of the Statue of Liberty.

Now answer Numbers 1 through 7 on your Answer Sheet. Base your answers on the changes Maria should make.

1 What is the best way to combine sentences 6 and 7?

A. Here I got to see and photograph the statue's original torch.

B. The statue's original torch I got to see and photograph it here.

C. Here I got to see, the statue's original torch, and here I got to photograph it.

D. The statue's original, torch was here for me to see and for me to photograph.

2 What change should be made in sentence 9?

F. change *taller* to **tallest**

G. delete the comma after *person*

H. change *person* to **people**

I. change the question mark to an exclamation point

3 What revision is needed in sentences 10 and 11?

A. We had to climb 354 steps, and not taking an elevator to reach the top.

B. Instead of taking an elevator to reach the top, we had to climb 354 steps.

C. Instead of taking the elevator to reach the top we climbed 354 steps instead.

D. Instead of taking an elevator to reach the top, and we had to climb 354 steps.

Name _____ Date _____

4 What change should be made in sentence 13?

F. change *steps* to **step**

G. change *hung* to **hanged**

H. delete the comma after *back*

I. change *procaution* to **precaution**

5 What change should be made in sentence 14?

A. change *It* to **It's**

B. change *was* to **were**

C. change *very much tiring* to **strenuous**

D. change *climb* to **climbed**

6 What is the best way to revise sentence 19?

F. All too soon we told a park ranger that we wanted to begin the descent, so I won't soon forget my experience inside the crown of the Statue of Liberty.

G. All too soon a park ranger told us that it was time to begin the descent, but I won't soon forget my experience inside the crown of the Statue of Liberty.

H. I won't soon forget my experience inside the crown of the Statue of Liberty, and all too soon us told a park ranger that it was time to begin the descent.

I. Because it was time to begin the descent, an all too soon park ranger told us, I won't soon forget my experience inside the crown of the Statue of Liberty.

7 Which sentence does NOT belong in this passage?

A. sentence 1

B. sentence 4

C. sentence 12

D. sentence 17

Name _____ Date _____

Read the introduction and the passage "Try New Things" before answering Numbers 8 through 13.

Avery wrote a passage about a difficult decision she made recently. Read her passage and think about the changes she should make.

Try New Things

(1) In the past, whenever someone would ask me what I liked to do, I would always say, "I'm a gymnast." (2) My gymnastics career only began when I was two years old, eleven years ago. (3) Growing up I spent countless hours at the gym, practicing my skills. (4) Many of my friends tried to convince me that I should try other things, such as softball or tennis.

(5) No one could appreciate my passion for the sport. (6) They couldn't comprehend the thrill of pulling off a complicated move after practicing it for months.

(7) Then shortly after my twelfth birthday something changed. (8) Suddenly I didn't spend my day looking forward to working on the balance beam, but competitions no longer excited me. (9) Instead some of my teammates and me dreaded them. (10) What was happening? (11) I wresled with my reluctance and persevered for a couple of months, but I just grew more and more unhappy.

(12) To relieve my frustration, I started going to the track to run with my mother. (13) One day we were finishing our run when a woman approached us. (14) She introduced herself as the middle school track coach and invited me to come to practice the next day.

(15) That evening, I called my gymnastics coach, and she encouraged me to meet with the track team. (16) At track practice I were able to try

new things. (17) I discovered that I was a fast runner, and my long jump

was superb! (18) I ended up quitting the gymnastics team, but not the sport.

(19) I still practice once a week, but I'm trying new things. (20) People still

ask me, "What's your favorite thing to do?" (21) These days I smile and say,

"I like to try new things."

_____

Now answer Numbers 8 through 13 on your Answer Sheet. Base your answers on the changes Avery should make.

8 What is the best way to revise sentence 2?

   F. My gymnastics career began eleven years ago, when I was only two years old.

   G. When I was two years old, eleven years ago, my only gymnastics career began.

   H. My gymnastics career when I was two years old began, only eleven years ago.

   I. When I was only two years old, my gymnastics career began eleven years ago.

9 What change should be made in sentence 7?

   A. change *after* to **over**

   B. change *my* to **mine**

   C. insert a comma after *birthday*

   D. change *something* to **Something**

10 What change should be made in sentence 8?

   F. change *spend* to **spent**

   G. delete the comma after *beam*

   H. change *but* to **and**

   I. change *me* to **I**

Name _____ Date _____

11 What change should be made in sentence 9?

A. change *Instead* to **Because**

B. change *dreaded* to **dreded**

C. change *me* to **I**

D. change *them* to **it**

12 What change should be made in sentence 11?

F. change *wresled* to **wrestled**

G. change *reluctance* to **reluctence**

H. delete the comma after *months*

I. change *but* to **so**

13 What change should be made in sentence 16?

A. change *At* to **Under**

B. change *practice* to **practicing**

C. change *were* to **was**

D. change *try* to **tried**

Read the introduction and the article "First Flight" before answering Numbers 14 through 19.

Anna wrote an article about a book she read. Read her article and think about the changes she should make.

First Flight

(1) I have always enjoying reading historical fiction. (2) I just finished reading *Seeing the First Flight* by Milton Nance. (3) It is a fantastick work of historical fiction. (4) In a new book, twelve-year-old Emily watches as Orville Wright makes the first airplane flight.

(5) Emily begins her story on the morning of the first flight. (6) Only a handful of people have gathered on the beach to witness history in the making. (7) Emily sees the Wright brothers flip a coin to determine who will attempt the first flight. (8) Orville, winning the coin toss, climbs onto the airplane. (9) Emily holds her breath as the plane lifts into the air for twelve seconds. (10) She watches it travel 120 feet. (11) The brothers then take turns flying the plane.

(12) Emily's thoughts are very much interesting. (13) She asks her if the airplane will transform the world. (14) She wonders if the american people will ever use airplanes for travel. (15) Through her thoughts and descriptions, readers catch a glimpse of the world before modern transportation. (16) I felt inspired to imagine the future of travel.

Name _____ Date _____

Now answer Numbers 14 through 19 on your Answer Sheet. Base your answers on the changes Anna should make.

14 What change should be made in sentence 1?

    F. change *have* to **had**

    G. change *enjoying* to **enjoyed**

    H. insert a comma after *reading*

    I. change *historical* to **Historical**

15 What change should be made in sentence 3?

    A. change *is* to **be**

    B. change *fantastick* to **fantastic**

    C. change *of* to **or**

    D. change the period to a question mark

16 What change should be made in sentence 4?

    F. change *a* to **this**

    G. change *twelve-year-old* to **Twelve-year-old**

    H. change *watches* to **had watched**

    I. change *makes* to **making**

17 What change should be made in sentence 12?

    A. change *Emily's* to **Emilys**

    B. change *are* to **is**

    C. change *very much interesting* to **fascinating**

    D. change the period to an exclamation point

Name _____ Date _____

18 What change should be made in sentence 13?

F. change *She* to **Her**

G. change *her* to **herself**

H. change *transform* to **tramsform**

I. change *world* to **World**

19 What change should be made in sentence 14?

A. change *wonders* to **wondering**

B. change *american* to **American**

C. change *will ever use* to **had ever used**

D. change the period to an exclamation point

Read the introduction and the passage "The Trip of a Lifetime" before answering Numbers 20 through 25.

Carlos wrote a passage about a child who visits relatives in another country. Read his passage and think about the changes he should make.

The Trip of a Lifetime

(1) Last summer, Adrian took a trip that most people only dream of taking. (2) He traveled to Germany with his parents to meet the family members he had only seen in pictures. (3) Adrian's parents who had come to the United States from Germany before Adrian was born, had told Adrian lots of stories about their German relatives. (4) I've been on a plane, but I've never traveled to Germany.

(5) The flight from the United States to Germany took more than ten hours. (6) Traveling by train from the airport, Adrian and his family reached they're relatives' home in the country in less than an hour. (7) Adrian's grandparents, aunts, uncles, and cousins were all waiting there, and they greeted Adrian as if they had known him all his life.

(8) The next day, the entire family went sightseeing in the Rhine River Valley. (9) The first stop was a castle that looked like it had been plucked from the pages of a fairy tale. (10) During a river cruise, the family saw many more castles, each with its own really very special history. (11) That night, the family sat on the riverbank and witnessed a magical fireworks show high above the water. (12) As his family watched the fireworks, Adrian thought it was the more happier time of his life. (13) Oh it would be difficult to say goodbye!

(14) Adrian and his parents look at pictures on the plane ride home when Adrian suddenly exclaimed, "That was the trip of a lifetime!"

(15) When Papa asked which part of the trip was his favorite, Adrian didn't hesitate to respond, "It was getting to spend time with our family."

Now answer Numbers 20 through 25 on your Answer Sheet. Base your answers on the changes Carlos should make.

20 What change should be made in sentence 3?

    F. change *Adrian's* to **Adrians'**

    G. insert a comma after *parents*

    H. change *had* to **have**

    I. delete the comma after *born*

21 What change should be made in sentence 10?

    A. delete the comma after *cruise*

    B. change *saw* to had **seen**

    C. change *really very special* to **unique**

    D. change the period to a question mark

22 What change should be made in sentence 12?

    F. change *As* to **So**

    G. change *watched* to **watches**

    H. change *was* to **were**

    I. change *more happier* to **happiest**

23 What change should be made in sentence 13?

    A. insert a comma after *Oh*

    B. change *difficult* to **difficulty**

    C. change *say* to **said**

    D. change the exclamation point to a question mark

24 What change should be made in sentence 14?

    F. change *look* to **were looking**

    G. change *when* to **while**

    H. delete the comma after *exclaimed*

    I. delete the quotation mark after the exclamation point

25 Which sentence does NOT belong in this passage?

    A. sentence 1

    B. sentence 4

    C. sentence 7

    D. sentence 11

STOP

Writing Arguments

Read the prompt and plan your response.

> Most people have a favorite book.
>
> Think about a favorite book and the reasons why you like it.
>
> Now write to persuade a friend to read your favorite book.

Planning Page

Use this space to make your notes before you begin writing. The writing on this page will NOT be scored.

_____

_____

_____

_____

_____

_____

_____

_____

_____

_____

_____

_____

_____

_____

**Begin writing your response here. The writing on this page and the next page
WILL be scored.**

_____

_____

_____

_____

_____

_____

_____

_____

_____

_____

_____

_____

_____

_____

_____

_____

_____

_____

_____

_____

_____

_____

Name _____ Date _____

_____

_____

_____

_____

_____

_____

_____

_____

_____

_____

_____

_____

_____

_____

_____

_____

_____

_____

_____

_____

_____

_____

_____

Reading Complex Text

Read the article "Mission to Mars: Moving Beyond Speculation." As you read, stop and answer each question. Use evidence from the article to support your answers.

Mission to Mars: Moving Beyond Speculation

Since the earliest written histories, people have been looking up into the skies and speculating about outer space. One of space's most tantalizing mysteries has always been one of its closest. Mars has long been the subject of fascination, especially for scientists. But Mars has not just captured the scientific imagination. It has also been the subject of many stories and movies. Most of these popular accounts of Mars revolve not just around what the planet looks like, but what type of life it might sustain.

Until the 20th century, the discussions about Mars were mostly speculation and fancy. No person or spacecraft had ever visited the planet. Telescopes could not provide images of the planet in great detail. Then, beginning in the 1960s, NASA, the U.S. agency responsible for space exploration, began launching missions to Mars. NASA sent spacecraft to circle the planet and take pictures and soil samples. These early missions put to rest the idea that intelligent or human-like Martians were in existence there. The pictures from early missions showed that Mars was extremely desolate and unlikely to support life. There seemed to be little to no water on the planet's surface. Mars's atmosphere appeared to be too thin to retain liquid water.

1 Why were discussions about Mars based only on speculation until relatively recently? Cite evidence from the text to support your answer.

_____

_____

_____

But the Mars missions raised more questions. Pictures confirmed that Mars's surface contained large canyons. These features indicate that water may have once been abundant on Mars, since canyons are usually formed by water movement. If water was once abundant on Mars, then Mars may, at one time, have held life. Although scientists were intrigued by the idea that Mars may have once held water and life, they also became concerned about what this meant for Earth. Could Earth's water and life also disappear?

Because of these new questions, scientists increased efforts to explore and understand Mars. Between 1960 and 1993, 19 space missions were sent to Mars. Unfortunately, in all that time, scientists were unable to really explore Mars's surface.

In the 1990s, scientists believed that in order to understand Mars, they needed to land a rover on the planet that could take sophisticated readings of the planet's soil and rocks.

Another concern was that missions to Mars were becoming increasingly expensive. This problem was highlighted by the 1993 failure of NASA's Mars Observer. Observer had taken eight years to build. It had cost nearly $1 billion. Furthermore, it was lost in space just days before it was scheduled to reach and orbit Mars. A small fuel leak caused an explosion that sent the Observer out beyond the reach of NASA's communications and controls. So, NASA began looking at ways to reduce the risks and costs of its missions while also better exploring Mars's surface.

2 How does the author help readers understand why NASA began looking to reduce the costs of missions to Mars?

_____

_____

_____

The agency turned to a team to develop an inexpensive rover to explore Mars's surface. The mission was called Pathfinder. In addition to landing a rover on Mars, the Pathfinder team was charged with finding inexpensive, creative ways of exploring Mars. Previous projects had employed hundreds of scientists to launch a Mars mission. This new team had 20 to 30 people. It was made up of scientists and engineers who embraced finding creative, cheap solutions to problems. Rather than building a bulky, powerful rover to explore Mars's surface, the team focused on building a small rover. At about 2 feet long and 1.5 feet wide, it weighed less than 25 pounds. The team also began using new technology, then being commonly used in laptops and cell phones, to develop the small rover. The rover was named "Sojourner," after civil rights heroine Sojourner Truth. In keeping costs, size, and weight low, the team eliminated many of the problems of transporting, landing, and operating a large Mars rover.

To keep costs low, the team sought out creative solutions to old problems. They had to think beyond traditional fixes and approach problems without prior ideas about how they had to be solved. For example, in the past, big, expensive rockets would have been used to slow down Sojourner as it began the drop onto Mars's surface. The Pathfinder team used a simple, far less expensive innovation: a parachute and air bags. Rather than using large batteries to power Sojourner, the rover was equipped with a small solar panel and ordinary flashlight batteries! Instead of designing all of the rover's components from scratch, the team used common antennas and motors. Then, the team modified them for use on Mars.

Name _____ Date _____

3 What evidence does the author give to support the claim that Sojourner's team looked for creative ways to solve old problems?

_____

_____

_____

When all was said and done, the Pathfinder mission cost $266 million. (Not a bad price for a complex mission!) Most importantly, however, the mission was a major success. On Friday, July 4, 1997, Sojourner and its landing unit, named Pathfinder, descended to Mars. After a successful landing, Sojourner and Pathfinder began exploring and analyzing the surface of Mars. The rover was guided by remote control from Earth. Sojourner and Pathfinder took photographs of the surface and analyzed the chemical make-up of the rocks on Mars's surface. Sojourner spent nearly three months exploring. During that time, Sojourner and the lander collected 2.6 billion bits of information. This included over 16,000 images, 15 chemical analyses of rocks and soil, and millions of reports on Martian weather. The Pathfinder mission proved that Mars exploration and study could be done more cheaply, and with fewer risks, than most scientists had previously imagined. As a result of the data collected during the mission, scientists confirmed that Mars once had conditions to support life! This was a major milestone in the scientific understanding of Mars. However many questions about Mars remain. Future missions will be necessary to learn more about the possibility or history of life on this mysterious and fascinating planet.

4 State the main idea of the article. How did the information about Sojourner and the Pathfinder mission convey this main idea?

_____

_____

_____

_____

_____

What evidence does the author give to support the claim that Sojourner's team looked for creative ways to solve old problems?

When all was said and done, the Pathfinder mission cost $266 million. (Not a bad price for a complex mission.) Most importantly, however, the mission was a major success. On Friday, July 4, 1997, Sojourner and its landing unit, named Pathfinder, descended to Mars. After a successful landing, Sojourner and Pathfinder began exploring and analyzing the surface of Mars. The rover was guided by remote control from Earth. Sojourner and Pathfinder took photographs of the surface and analyzed the chemical make-up of the rocks on Mars's surface. Sojourner spent nearly three months exploring. During that time, Sojourner and the lander collected 2.6 billion bits of information. This included over 16,000 images, 15 chemical analyses of rocks and soil, and millions of reports on Martian weather. The Pathfinder mission proved that Mars exploration and study could be done more cheaply, and with fewer risks, than most scientists had previously imagined. As a result of the data collected during the mission, scientists confirmed that Mars once had conditions to support life! This was a major milestone in the scientific understanding of Mars. However many questions about Mars remain. Future missions will be necessary to learn more about the possibility or history of life on this mysterious and fascinating planet.

State the main idea of the article. How did the information about Sojourner and the Pathfinder mission convey this main idea?

Reading and Analyzing Text

Read the passage "Project Frog" and the instructions "How to Create a Homemade
Wetland" before answering Numbers 1 through 17.

Project Frog

After spreading out and counting the money she had saved, Cecilia groaned, pretty
sure that $63 wouldn't save many frogs.

Cecilia's mother looked up from her work and asked, "Are you thinking of buying
something?"

"I'm trying to figure out whether or not I can help protect frogs," said Cecilia.
"We learned in school that frogs around the world are dying. It's a huge problem, and
unfortunately, my cash supply is anything *but* huge."

"Maybe you could pass out informative flyers to educate people about the issue,"
said her mom, trying to be supportive.

Cecilia considered the idea, but she wasn't sure that passing out flyers would get the
kind of results she wanted. She wanted to do something interesting and unique to get
people's attention. Cecilia was determined to take action and get other people to do the
same. She headed to her computer in hopes of finding some inspiration. As she read
article after article on the Internet, Cecilia jotted down notes on what she learned about
the frog problem:

- *The growing human population has led to more building and more pollution,
  both of which can have fatal consequences for frogs.*

- *Clearing of land and building new structures have destroyed much frog habitat.*

- *Pesticides and weed killers used in farming can wash into streams and ponds
  where frogs live. Scientific data shows that these chemicals increase stress in
  frogs, making them less able to fight off disease.*

- *A deadly skin fungus is wiping out frogs at an alarming rate. Scientists say
  that global warming has created conditions that allow the fungus to grow out
  of control.*

Finally Cecilia found a website that gave her a great idea.

"Mom," she said excitedly, "I know how to get people involved. I just need a few
supplies from the hardware store and a couple of friends to help me build a model."

"A model of what?" asked her mother.

Name _____ Date _____

"Of this," answered Cecilia, handing her mother a printout with instructions for building a homemade wetland for frogs.

Her mother read the instructions and agreed that a homemade wetland would be a good way for Cecilia to use her limited resources. Her mom even offered to share the expenses. "But how will this mobilize[1] other people?" she asked.

"We can pass out flyers to the neighbors advertising a class to be held in our backyard," said Cecilia. "People can see our model and learn how to do the same thing in their yard. It would not only help frogs but also look terrific!"

The next day, Cecilia and her mother bought the supplies. After Cecilia marked out the location for her backyard wetland, her friends helped her dig the hole, and Cecilia's mom helped them install the plastic liner. Finally, they filled the pond with water and planted water lilies, grass, and ferns in and around the pond.

Cecilia thought the finished wetland looked like a great habitat for amphibians; she could hardly wait for the frogs to find it. In the meantime, she got to work making flyers and writing the project instructions she would explain in her class. She had the thrilling feeling that she was actually going to make a difference!

[1]**mobilize:** put into action

How to Create a Homemade Wetland

The simple steps below explain how you can create a great home for frogs that is also an attractive water feature for your yard.

Materials

Gather these items: rope or a garden hose, shovels, rocks of various sizes, several bags of sand, a plastic liner made specifically for ponds, water plants, ferns, grasses.

Planning

First, get your parents' permission to create a homemade wetland. Ask them for guidance in choosing the right place for the pond. Then, use the rope or garden hose to mark the pond's shape and location. Remember that tadpoles cannot survive in full sun, so part of the pond should be shaded.

Site Preparation

Dig out the hole for your pond so that it has a shallow end and a deep end. The deepest part should go down about three feet. The other end should be shallow enough to stay muddy and bog-like. The sides should be gently sloped so amphibians can easily crawl in and out.

Building the Pond

Spread a layer of wet sand about two inches thick over the pond bottom. The sand will provide a cushion that protects the plastic pond liner from being punctured by rocks.

Inspect your pond liner thoroughly to make sure it doesn't have any holes. You must use a liner that is made especially for ponds because other kinds of plastic can break down and be toxic[2] to wildlife.

Spread the liner over the sand, smooth it into place, and anchor it with rocks or bricks. Then bury the outer edges of the liner under six inches of soil. Add decorative pebbles and stones around the rim and fill the pond with water.

Planting

Let the pond water stand for three days to allow any chlorine to evaporate before you proceed with planting. Next, place large rocks and logs on the bottom of the pond and plant water lilies and other aquatic plants around them. Plants should cover more than half of the surface area of the pond. Having plenty of plants will slow the growth of algae and prevent your pond from becoming dirty or stagnant.

Along the muddy edge of the pond and in the shallow end of the pool, plant plenty of grasses and ferns where frogs can eat insects and lay eggs and where tadpoles can feed and hide.

Caution

Once your pond is ready, it may take a while for native frogs to discover it. Do not get impatient and buy frogs to add to your pond, or you could make frog decline worse! Frogs brought in from other places often eat native frogs and take over a local habitat.

[2]**toxic:** harmful or poisonous

Now answer Numbers 1 through 17 on your Answer Sheet. Base your answers
on the passage "Project Frog" and the instructions "How to Create a Homemade
Wetland."

1 Why is Cecilia frustrated at the beginning of the passage?

   A. She can't find instructions for building a pond.

   B. Her school isn't doing anything to protect frogs.

   C. Her mother doesn't understand what Cecilia's goal is.

   D. She doesn't have enough money to accomplish very much.

2 Read this sentence from the passage "Project Frog."

> **"I'm trying to figure out whether or not I can help protect frogs,"
> said Cecilia.**

Which word is a homophone for the word *whether* in the sentence above?

   F. waiter

   G. weather

   H. wherever

   I. wither

3 Read this sentence from the passage "Project Frog."

> **"Maybe you could pass out informative flyers to educate people about
> the issue," said her mom, trying to be supportive.**

What does the word *informative* mean in the sentence above?

   A. seeking information

   B. being well-informed

   C. providing information

   D. collecting information

Name _____ Date _____

4 Cecilia thought that passing out flyers

  F. wouldn't get people to take action.

  G. wouldn't get support from her friends.

  H. would require too much help from her mom.

  I. would use too much paper and take too much time.

5 Read this sentence from the passage "Project Frog."

  "Maybe you could pass out informative flyers to educate people about the issue," said her mom, trying to be supportive.

  What does the word *supportive* mean in the sentence above?

  A. creative

  B. encouraging

  C. patient

  D. youthful

6 Read this sentence from the passage "Project Frog."

  She wanted to do something interesting and unique to get people's attention.

  Which word has the same sound as the underlined letter in *unique*?

  F. carnival

  G. guessing

  H. juicy

  I. league

7 Read this sentence from the passage "Project Frog."

> *The growing human population has led to more building and more pollution, both of which can have fatal consequences for frogs.*

What does the word *consequences* mean in the sentence above?

A. pollutants

B. results

C. rewards

D. warnings

8 Which words best describe Cecilia's attitude toward helping frogs?

F. outraged and upset

G. earnest and energetic

H. interested and amused

I. light-hearted and casual

9 Read this sentence from the passage "Project Frogs."

> **Scientists say that global warming has created conditions that allow the fungus to grow out of control.**

What does the word *conditions* mean in the sentence above?

A. illnesses

B. problems

C. situations

D. worries

10 In the instructions "How to Create a Homemade Wetland," under which subheading can readers find information about the correct depth for a frog pond?

F. Planning

G. Site Preparation

H. Planting

I. Caution

11 Read this sentence about the instructions "How to Create a Homemade Wetland."

> **The instructions direct kids to have their parents _____ them about where to make a pond.**

Which word best completes the sentence above?

A. adjust

B. advice

C. advise

D. affect

12 Read this sentence from the instructions "How to Create a Homemade Wetland."

> **Remember that tadpoles cannot survive in full sun, so part of the pond should be shaded.**

Now complete this analogy, based on the sentence above: *full sun* is to *tadpoles* as "dry air" is to

F. birds.

G. fish.

H. insects.

I. plants.

13 Cecilia's pond is most likely to become dirty and stagnant if she

A. uses too few plants.

B. makes the pond too wide.

C. slopes the sides of the pond.

D. buys frogs to add to her pond.

14 Based on the instructions "How to Create a Homemade Wetland," the reader can conclude that a pond will only help increase the local frog population if it

F. attracts frogs right away.

G. has more water lilies than grass.

H. is located in an area with full sun.

I. includes a shallow area with plants.

15 Read this sentence from the passage "How to Create a Homemade Wetland."

> **Do not get impatient and buy frogs to add to your pond, or you could make frog decline worse!**

What does the word *impatient* mean?

A. patented

B. with a pat

C. not patient

D. very patient

16 Read this sentence about the instructions "How to Create a Homemade Wetland."

> **Spreading a layer of sand is the step that _____ installing the pond liner.**

Which word correctly completes the sentence above?

F. precedes

G. presides

H. proceeds

I. processes

17 Both the passage "Project Frog" and the instructions "How to Create a Homemade Wetland" include information about

A. threats to the survival of frogs.

B. habitat requirements of tadpoles.

C. the correct depth for a frog pond.

D. organizing a pond-building class.

Read the article "Dreams for Sale" and Posters 1 and 2 before answering Numbers 18 through 35.

Dreams for Sale

When a carpenter noticed a bit of yellow metal in a river in California, he started a wild chapter in American history. The year was 1848. The carpenter, a man named James Marshall, was building a mill for John Sutter along the American River. While working, Marshall's crew found gold by merely scratching the riverbank with a knife! Elated at their good fortune, they spread the word that there was a wealth of gold at Sutter's Mill. At first, most people regarded the claims as empty rumors. Eventually, a few tried their luck and returned with plump pouches of gold. Once people saw proof that the claims were true, word spread quickly. The city of San Francisco practically emptied out and closed down as its citizens invaded the Sutter's Mill area with picks and shovels in hand. The Gold Rush had begun!

While people all along the west coast were leaving their homes to look for gold, those back East received the news warily. It wasn't until a government worker published an official report and sent a boxful of gold to Washington that gold fever spread through the whole country. People abandoned all feelings of caution once they learned the claims were proven. In their rush to strike it rich, people began to believe anything and everything they were told. After all, if there was proof that gold was floating in the rivers and lying on the ground all over California, anything might be true!

Name _____ Date _____

Many trusting people became victims of scam artists. Dishonest merchants[1] took advantage of people's hopeful thinking. They made wild claims and false promises. Some guaranteed a quick and luxurious passage to the gold fields by carriage, ship, or wagon. One man claimed he had invented a flying machine that could repel bow and arrow attacks. He promised to get travelers to California in three days. In truth, there was no flying machine and almost all journeys to California were long, difficult, and dangerous.

Some merchants raised their prices for tools, guns, and anything else miners might buy. They got customers to spend money on useless gadgets by claiming that they were necessary for mining gold. One merchant even advertised a miraculous grease. It came with the promise that when rubbed onto the skin it would attract gold dust and make it stick to a miner's body!

Other people made a profit by selling information. They gave phony tips about the trip west or about gold-mining. They portrayed themselves as experts and sold books, maps, and tickets to lectures. Many of these so-called experts hadn't even been to California! In spite of their greedy motives, they always drew a crowd. They were masters at telling people what they wanted to hear. One speaker promised to reveal the sites of secret gold mines. Another declared that miners could make a thousand dollars a day. He insisted they could extract a half an ounce of gold from just one handful of dirt. One mythmaker claimed he had found huge chunks of pure gold. He described one as being the width of both his hands put together! As improbable as these tales were, gold-hungry crowds readily believed them. Most of the Gold Rush guidebooks made their authors rich while misleading those who read them.

Posters similar to the ones on the following pages publicized services for would-be gold miners. The ads were written to appeal to people's dreams of finding an easy fortune in the West.

[1]**merchants:** people who purchase, sell, or trade goods for profit

212

Poster 1

CALIFORNIA BOUND!
Ride the *Silver Stage*
Take the Easy Road to Fortune!

Having outfitted this coach to suit the most discriminating traveler,
Silver Stage Travel Co.
is now offering comfortable passage to the richest gold fields in California.

Will depart the 3rd of March with luxurious accommodations and meals for the lucky travelers who are first to book passage.

Good-natured, experienced drivers devote every attention to your comfort and safety.

Explore the frontier in worry-free comfort while your parlor on wheels transports you over smooth, safe roads.

For further particulars, see
Martin D. Crawford, Agent

Poster 2

Richest Mines
in

CALIFORNIA!!
Gold Mining Secrets

will be revealed by

J. D. Morse

A foremost expert on locating gold in California

Mr. Morse, who has experienced firsthand the discovery of large lumps of pure gold ore, will deliver a

L E C T U R E

At 7 in the evening in the Town Hall
on the 5th day of April, 1849.

F O R T U N E

awaits those who follow the instructions and advice of this well-informed guide. Your speaker will share his personal success story. Only he can provide the reliable information you have been seeking. He will recommend the best routes, camps, and mining destinations. As well, he will offer advice on provisions and gear. For a small fee, your speaker will furnish you with a map that shows the location of rich, but unexploited

SECRET MINES!!

Name _____ Date _____

Now answer Numbers 18 through 35 on your Answer Sheet. Base your answers on the article "Dreams for Sale" and Posters 1 and 2.

18 Read this sentence from the article.

> **Eventually, a few tried their luck and returned with plump pouches of gold.**

In the sentence above, the word *eventually* means

   F. eagerly

   G. nervously

   H. right away

   I. after a while

19 What is the main idea of the second paragraph of the article?

   A. Easterners were more cautious than Westerners.

   B. Gold was lying on the ground all over California.

   C. A government report caused gold fever to spread.

   D. People joined the Gold Rush without hearing any reports.

20 Read this sentence from the article.

> **While people all along the west coast were leaving their homes to look for gold, those back East received the news warily.**

What does the word *warily* mean in the sentence above?

   F. in a hopeful way

   G. in a cautious way

   H. in an astonished way

   I. in a disinterested way

Name _____ Date _____

21 Read this sentence from the article.

Many trusting people became victims of scam artists.

What does the word *victims* mean in the sentence above?

A. people who study

B. people who bother

C. people who are helped

D. people who are tricked

22 What information might have persuaded people to buy one merchant's miraculous grease?

F. the grease's ability to help people travel faster

G. a promise that the grease would make people fly

H. a promise that the grease would attract gold dust

I. the grease's ability to repel bow and arrow attacks

23 Read this sentence from the article.

In spite of their greedy motives, they always drew a crowd.

What does the word *motives* mean in the sentence above?

A. feelings

B. profits

C. purposes

D. reputations

24 Based on the article, the reader can conclude that many scam artists got rich during the Gold Rush because there was a

F. large supply of gold, but no way to get it.

G. great desire for odd gadgets, but very few suppliers.

H. large number of newly rich miners, but not much to buy.

I. great demand for information, but not many facts available.

216

25 Read this sentence from the article.

> **One speaker promised to reveal the sites of secret gold mines.**

Which word is a homophone for the word *sites* in the sentence above?

A. cities

B. kites

C. sights

D. sits

26 Read this sentence from the article.

> **He insisted they could extract a half an ounce of gold from just one handful of dirt.**

What does the word *extract* mean?

F. to put in

G. to pull out

H. to create for

I. to write about

27 Read this sentence from the article.

> **One mythmaker claimed he had found huge chunks of pure gold.**

What does the word *mythmaker* mean?

A. a person from the past

B. a person who likes nature

C. a person who creates stories

D. a person who studies cultures

28 Read this sentence from the article.

> As improbable as these tales were, gold-hungry crowds readily
> believed them.

What does the word *improbable* mean?

F. not probable

G. not very able

H. most probable

I. tending to babble

29 Which statement expresses the false promise that some Gold Rush guidebook authors
hoped their readers would believe?

A. "For a small fee, I will sell you a book and a map."

B. "For a small amount of money, I will make you rich."

C. "For a few minutes of your time, I will entertain you."

D. "For a share of your profits later, I will give you free advice."

30 Information in the article supports the generalization that the promise of wealth

F. is always a false promise.

G. only appeals to foolish people.

H. helps most people find happiness.

I. can cause people to use poor judgment.

31 Read this sentence from the article.

> Posters similar to the ones on the following pages publicized services for
> would-be gold miners.

What does the word *publicized* mean in the sentence above?

A. surprised the public

B. questioned the public

C. made known to the public

D. took money from the public

Name _____   Date _____

32   Read this excerpt from Poster 1.

Explore the frontier in worry-free comfort while your parlor on wheels transports you over smooth, safe roads.

What does the word *transports* mean in the sentence above?

F. carries

G. leads

H. pushes

I. shows

33   In Poster 1, how do interested customers get prices for the Silver Stage service?

A. Wait for March 3.

B. Contact the agent listed.

C. Speak with the driver of the coach.

D. Look for the correct stagecoach in town.

34   Which feature of Poster 2 helps the reader know what kind of information audiences can expect to hear?

F. The name of the lecturer is near the top of the ad.

G. The word *lecture* is in larger type than other words.

H. Words related to getting rich are in capitalized letters.

I. The time and location are right below the word *lecture*.

35   Read this sentence about the article.

Scam artists caused a lot of trusting people to _____ their money.

Which word correctly completes the sentence above?

A. loose

B. lose

C. loss

D. lost

Name _____ Date _____

Revising and Editing

Read the introduction and the passage "My Bird Paradise" before answering Numbers 1 through 7.

Michael wrote this passage about the bird-friendly backyard he and his family created. Read his passage and think about the changes he should make.

My Bird Paradise

(1) Last summer my dad suggested that, "We transform our backyard into an inviting place for birds." (2) Dad and I got helpful information from a book called Building a Bird Paradise. (3) We followed the author's instructions. (4) We planted trees and shrubs that produce berries and nuts. (5) Then we hung feeders near trees so birds could hide if they felt they were in danger. (6) We also put out two birdbaths so our visitors could drink without being crowded. (7) Last, we put a bell on our cat. (8) That way the birds could hear him coming.

(9) I clean and refill the birdbaths every day so standing water won't cause a mosqeto problem. (10) My parents clean and fill the feeders.

Name _____ Date _____

(11) Dad's in charge of the feeders that hold seeds and Mom puts food in the hummingbird feeders.

   (12) Now we spend most evenings on the back porch, watching birds. (13) It's a challenge to try to identify the bird sounds we hear. (14) At first I wasn't familiar with any of the bird calls, but I'm slowly getting better at identifying them. (15) Now I always recognize the soft, cooing sound of a dove, the cheerful whistling sound of a cardinal, and the shrill screaming sound of a blue jay. (16) Someday I hope I can identify every bird that visits our backyard paradise.

Now answer Numbers 1 through 7 on your Answer Sheet. Base your answers on the changes Michael should make.

1 What is the best way to revise sentence 1?

A. Last summer, my dad suggested, "We transform our backyard into an inviting place for birds."

B. Last summer, my dad suggested that we transform our backyard into an inviting place for birds.

C. Last summer, my dad suggested that. We transform our backyard into an inviting place for birds.

D. Last summer, my dad suggested, "That we transform our backyard into an inviting place for birds."

2 What change should be made in sentence 2?

F. change *I* to **me**

G. change *got* to **gotten**

H. insert a comma after *book*

I. type in italics *Building a Bird Paradise*

3 Which sentence could best be added before sentence 9?

    A. Mom recognizes more bird calls than Dad and I do.

    B. Mom, Dad, and I all work to maintain our bird-friendly yard.

    C. I never knew that bird-watching could be so much fun.

    D. We don't want insects to overtake the paradise we created.

4 What change should be made in sentence 9?

    F. change *refill* to **refills**

    G. insert a comma after *day*

    H. change *won't* to **didn't**

    I. change *mosqeto* to **mosquito**

5 What change should be made in sentence 11?

    A. change *Dad's* to **Dads**

    B. change *hold* to **holds**

    C. insert a comma after *seeds*

    D. change *Mom* to **mom**

6 What change should be made in sentence 14?

    F. change *At* to **In**

    G. insert a comma after *first*

    H. change *familiar* to **familiur**

    I. change *slowly* to **slow**

7 What is the best way to revise sentence 15?

A. Now I always recognize the soft, cooing sound of a dove; the cheerful, whistling sound of a cardinal; and the shrill, screaming sound of a blue jay.

B. Now I always recognize the soft; cooing sound of a dove, the cheerful; whistling sound of a cardinal, and the shrill screaming sound of a blue jay.

C. Now I always recognize the soft cooing sound, of a dove, the cheerful whistling sound, of a cardinal, and the shrill screaming sound, of a blue jay.

D. Now I always recognize the soft, cooing, sound of a dove: the cheerful, whistling sound, of a cardinal: and the shrill, screaming sound, of a blue jay.

Read the introduction and the passage "My Favorite Legend" before answering Numbers 8 through 13.

Katy wrote this passage about her favorite Native American legend. Read her passage and think about the changes she should make.

My Favorite Legend

(1) My grandmother, the greatest storyteller I know told me the following legend. (2) It comes from the mythelogy of the Papago people. (3) The story may have other names, but Grandmother calls it "When Butterflies Were Born."

(4) One late summer's day, the Creator was enjoying the beautiful world he had made. (5) He smiled with satisfaction at the brilliant blue of the sky and the colorful clothing of children who were playing in the sunshine. (6) Nearby, the mothers of the children were grinding corn to store for the winter. (7) The lovely whiteness of the cornmeal brought another smile of contentment to the Creator's face. (8) Most delightful of all were the much bright colors of the summer flowers in the gardens all around.

(9) As the Creator thought about the coming change in the seasons, tears sprang to his eyes, for he realized that the sky would soon fade from blue to gray, and the children would put on their dull-colored coats. (10) The lovely white cornmeal would be hidden away in jars and the flowers would wither from their stems.

(11) Suddenly, the Creator was struck by a wonderful idea. (12) I will preserve all the vibrant colors of this day, he exclaimed, so that they will never fade from memory!

Name _____ Date _____

(13) He collected flowers of yellow, orange, purple, and crimson and put them in a bag. (14) Next he mixed in blue from the sky, white from the cornmeal and all the playful colors from the children's clothing. (15) Finally, he offered his new creation to the children, who eagerly opened the bag. (16) To everyone's delight, amazing colors flew out and seemed to float on the air. (17) This is how the first butterflies were born!

Now answer Numbers 8 through 13 on your Answer Sheet. Base your answers on the changes Katy should make.

8 What change should be made in sentence 1?

   F. change *grandmother* to **Grandmother**

   G. insert a comma after *know*

   H. change *legend* to **Legend**

   I. change the period to an exclamation point

9 What change should be made in sentence 2?

   A. change *comes* to **come**

   B. change *mytholegy* to **mythology**

   C. change *Papago* to **papago**

   D. change the period to a question mark

10 What change should be made in sentence 8?

   F. change *Most* to **More**

   G. change *delightful* to **delight**

   H. change *were* to **was**

   I. change *much bright* to **brilliant**

11 What change should be made in sentence 10?

    A. change *would* to **wood**

    B. change *hidden* to **hided**

    C. insert a comma after *jars*

    D. change *and* to **but**

12 What is the best way to revise sentence 12?

    F. "I will preserve all the vibrant colors of this day, he exclaimed, so that they will never fade from memory!"

    G. "I will preserve all the vibrant colors of this day," he exclaimed, "so that they will never fade from memory!"

    H. "I will preserve all the vibrant colors of this day." He exclaimed, "so that they will never fade from memory!"

    I. "I will preserve all the vibrant colors of this day" he exclaimed "so that they will never fade from memory!"

13 What change should be made in sentence 14?

    A. change *blue* to **blew**

    B. insert a comma after *cornmeal*

    C. change *playful* to **playfull**

    D. change *children's* to **childrens'**

Name _____ Date _____

Read the introduction and the article "A Mystery with a Twist" before answering Numbers 14 through 19.

Don wrote this article about a mystery story that he read. Read his article and think about the changes he should make.

A Mystery with a Twist

(1) The Case of the Creepy Garage is the fifth book in the Freddy Franklin mystery series. (2) In this latest book, a mysterious man and his wife who move in next door arouse Freddy's suspicions.

(3) Day after day, bumping sounds wake Freddy before sunrise, but all he can see is an eerie light flashing in the neighbors' garage. (4) The young sleuth, hoping to expoze a brilliant crime, starts taking notes. (5) He carefully observes the pre-dawn activities of his neighbor, or Dr. Darkness, as Freddy begins to call him. (6) After sunrise, the man leaves his house in a truck, with a tarp over a large load in the back. (7) When he returns the truck is always empty. (8) Meanwhile, the man's wife never appears and her red car never leaves the driveway. (9) Freddy tries to convince his parents that something illegal is going on but they dismiss his far-fetched theories about a smuggling ring.

(10) The climax occurs early one morning when the neighbors leave in a rush. (11) They throw a suitcase into the red car and speed away, leaving the garage door wide open. (12) Freddy insists that they are headed to Las Vegas Nevada, with a suitcase full of loot. (13) His exasperated dad asks what will it take to convince you that you're imagining all this?

Name _____ Date _____

(14) When Freddy pleads for just one look inside the open garage,

his dad reluctantly agrees. (15) When they peer in the garage, they see

thousands of worms writhing and squirming in the back of the truck!

(16) I won't explain everything, but I'll give you three clues. (17) Some

people raise earthworms to sell, earthworms will do anything to stay out

of the light, and people hurry when a baby is on the way!

(18) This is the first book in which Freddy is wrong, and I really

liked the unexpected ending. (19) I like mysteries by other authors, too.

(20) Freddy I can't wait to read your next mystery! (21) Maybe you'll learn

to go over and meet your new neighbors!

Now answer Numbers 14 through 19 on your Answer Sheet. Base your answers on the changes Don should make.

14 What change should be made in sentence 1?

    F. type in italics *The Case of the Creepy Garage*

    G. change *fifth* to **five**

    H. change *Franklin* to **franklin**

    I. change *series* to **serious**

15 What change should be made in sentence 4?

    A. change *hoping* to **hopes**

    B. change *expoze* to **expose**

    C. change *starts* to **start**

    D. change *taking* to **taken**

228

Name _____ Date _____

16 What change should be made in sentence 12?

    F. change *insists* to **insisted**

    G. insert a comma after *Las Vegas*

    H. change *Nevada* to **nevada**

    I. change *of* to **in**

17 What is the best way to revise sentence 13?

    A. His exasperated dad asks, "What will it take to convince you that you're imagining all this"?

    B. His exasperated dad "asks What will it take to convince you that you're imagining all this"?

    C. His exasperated dad asks, "What will it take to convince you that you're imagining all this?"

    D. His exasperated dad asks: What will it take to convince you that "you're imagining all this?"

18 What change should be made in sentence 20?

    F. insert a comma after *Freddy*

    G. change *can't* to **ca'nt**

    H. change *wait* to **weight**

    I. change *your* to **you're**

19 Which sentence does NOT belong in this passage?

    A. sentence 3

    B. sentence 7

    C. sentence 14

    D. sentence 19

Read the introduction and the article "Dark Days of the Dust Bowl" before answering Numbers 20 through 25.

Ana wrote this article about the Dust Bowl. Read her article and think about the changes she should make.

Dark Days of the Dust Bowl

(1) In 1930, a drought began in the United States and spread slowly across the central part of the country. (2) By 1934, it had turned America's grassy lands into a dessert. (3) Along with poor farming methods, this brought on the really super bad years of the Dust Bowl.

(4) It wasn't until 1935 that the driest part of the country got the name "Dust Bowl." (5) Robert Geiger, a reporter who traveled through the area, first used the term. (6) The Dust Bowl included these areas western Kansas, southeastern Colorado, the Oklahoma Panhandle, the Texas Panhandle, and northeastern New Mexico. (7) Another reporter who toured the Dust Bowl wrote, it is the saddest land I have ever seen.

(8) The Dust Bowl was especially difficult for those who lived on farms that disappeared under a blanket of dust. (9) Their life was made miserable by intense dust storms black blizzards that turned sunny days into complete darkness. (10) The dust buried tractors and cars. (11) It blew in through every door, window, and crack in a house.

(12) Seventy years later, those who survived the Dust Bowl remember those days clearly. (13) Their memoirs are filled with details that sound like science fiction. (14) In an article entitled Dust Bowl Stories," one person described tying a towel over her nose and mouth every day to keep

Name _____ Date _____

from getting sick. (15) Once, when caught in a storm, she covered her whole head and hung onto a fence to keep from blowing away!

(16) Though the drought years of the Dust Bowl ended around 1941, memories of those difficult days have not faded.

Now answer Numbers 20 through 25 on your Answer Sheet. Base your answers on the changes Ana should make.

20 What change should be made in sentence 2?

F. change *turned* to **turn**

G. change *America's* to **america's**

H. change *grassy* to **grassly**

I. change *dessert* to **desert**

21 What change should be made in sentence 3?

A. change the comma to a colon

B. change *brought* to **bring**

C. change *really super bad* to **terrible**

D. insert a comma after *years*

22 What change should be made in sentence 6?

F. change *included* to **include**

G. insert a colon after *areas*

H. change *and* to **or**

I. change *New* to **new**

23 What is the best way to revise sentence 7?

   A. Another reporter who toured the Dust Bowl wrote. It is the saddest land I have ever seen.

   B. Another reporter who toured the Dust Bowl wrote "It is the saddest land I have ever seen."

   C. Another reporter who toured the Dust Bowl wrote It is the saddest land I have ever seen.

   D. Another reporter who toured the Dust Bowl wrote, "It is the saddest land I have ever seen."

24 What change should be made in sentence 9?

   F. change *Their* to **There**

   G. change *miserable* to **miserible**

   H. insert parentheses around *black blizzards*

   I. change the period to a question mark

25 What change should be made in sentence 14?

   A. change *an* to **a**

   B. insert a quotation mark before *Dust*

   C. change *tying* to **tieing**

   D. change *getting* to **get**

Name _____ Date _____

Writing to Narrate

Most people have had an experience that caused them to change the way they feel or think about something.

Think of an experience you had that caused you to change the way you feel or think about something.

Now write a personal narrative about an experience you had that made you change the way you feel or think about something.

Planning Page

Use this space to make your notes before you begin writing. The writing on this page will NOT be scored.

Name _____ Date _____

**Begin writing your response here. The writing on this page and the next page
WILL be scored.**

_____

_____

_____

_____

_____

_____

_____

_____

_____

_____

_____

_____

_____

_____

_____

_____

_____

_____

_____

_____

_____

Name _____ Date _____

_____

_____

_____

_____

_____

_____

_____

_____

_____

_____

_____

_____

_____

_____

_____

_____

_____

_____

_____

_____

_____

_____

_____

_____

Reading Complex Text

Read the passage "An Odd-Tasting Banana." As you read, stop and answer each question. Use evidence from the passage to support your answers.

An Odd-Tasting Banana

Arely and I burst through the door of her family's apartment, heaping our backpacks, coats, and gear from soccer practice into a corner.

"I'm so hungry!" I exclaimed at the same moment that Arely declared, "I'm so filthy!" We burst out laughing, as Arely stood back to display her mud-spattered legs. As our team's goalie, Arely had taken more than one diving leap into a mud puddle to prevent a ball from entering the goal. She had emerged from practice a muddy mess.

"I'm going to take a quick shower before we start our homework, Christina. Please help yourself to anything you can find for a snack," Arely told me, heading down the hall toward the bathroom.

"Thanks!" I said. A bowl on the counter held a rainbow assortment of fresh fruits, several of which I did not recognize. I picked up and inspected an odd-looking, grapefruit-sized piece of fruit whose yellow flesh was covered in tiny bumps. Underneath was a bulbous green fruit, speckled pink in spots. A mango, perhaps? It was funny to think about how different the Lopez's fruit bowl looked compared to my own family's fruit bowl, which contained our household's staples—apples, oranges, and bananas. Though intrigued by these tropical, exotic-looking fruits, I didn't have the faintest notion of how to go about eating them. So instead I grabbed a piece of fruit that I recognized: a banana.

---

1 Why does Christina choose a banana from the Lopez's fruit bowl? What evidence from the passage supports your answer?

_____

_____

_____

The banana was slightly green, but I much preferred an under-ripe banana to an overripe, brown-freckled banana. I tugged and tugged at the stem, bending it this way and that way in an attempt to remove the peel. Like a determined goalie,

Name _____ Date _____

however, it resisted all of my efforts. Taking a deep breath, I finally wrenched off the banana's stem and peeled back the resilient skin. And then I took a bite.

I had never minded the firm texture and starchy sweet taste of an under-ripe banana, but this banana was downright hard, bitter-tasting, and not the least bit sweet. In fact, it tasted more like what I imagined a raw potato would be like.

The expression on my face must have been priceless as I stood contemplating whether to swallow the odd-tasting banana or spit it out. A loud peal of laughter startled me. I glanced up to find Arely's mother standing in the doorway, clutching a brown grocery sack in one hand and trying to cover her laughter with the other hand.

"Christina, I didn't mean to startle you, and I'm certainly not making fun of you. I'm just sorry you had to find out the hard way that an unripe plantain is best enjoyed cooked, not raw!"

I grimaced, forcing myself to swallow. "I was just beginning to think that maybe this wasn't a banana after all! What is a plantain, Mrs. Lopez?"

---

2 How does the scene above explain the conflict in the passage?

_____

_____

_____

"A plantain is a sibling to the banana, but a raw plantain is typically cooked. Where I'm from in Puerto Rico, we sometimes refer to plantains as 'cooking bananas' and regular bananas as 'dessert bananas.' Cooking raw plantains brings out their flavor," Mrs. Lopez told me as she hung up her coat and began unpacking groceries.

"Did I overhear that Christina just bit into a raw green plantain?" Arely asked, emerging from the hallway.

I grinned sheepishly at my friend and shrugged my shoulders.

"Arely, I think it's only fair that we make it up to Christina by preparing for her a delicious, authentic Puerto Rican plantain snack. What do you think?" Mrs. Lopez raised her dark eyebrows at her daughter, who nodded enthusiastically.

Seizing the bunch of plantains from the bowl, Arely declared, "Just wait, Christina! When you taste a plantain prepared by Mamá and me, you'll forget all about the unpleasant experience of eating a raw green plantain!"

> **3**   What does Mrs. Lopez mean by "a plantain is a sibling to the banana"?
>
> _____
>
> _____
>
> _____

Arely's mother laughed at her animated daughter. "Since our plantains are unripe," she said, "let's slice them up and make baked *tostones* for Christina." Mrs. Lopez turned and said, "In Puerto Rico, *tostones* are most often fried, but Arely and I enjoy them baked just as well."

I watched as Arely and her mother trimmed the ends of the plantains and then sliced the peel lengthwise to remove the tough outer skin. Next, Arely's mother cut the fruit into half-inch thick slices and transferred these to a bowl. Arely tossed the plantain pieces with a little bit of oil and salt and arranged them on a baking sheet.

As the *tostones* were baking, Arely told me all about her grandmother, Abuela, who still lived in Puerto Rico. Arely stayed with Abuela all of last summer when she visited with her parents.

The kitchen was beginning to fill with a scent like roasted potatoes, except it was tinged with sweetness. "Mmmmmmm . . . the *tostones* smell delicious!" I said, breathing in the wonderful aroma. Arely's mother pulled a tray of slightly browned plantain slices from the oven and laid it to rest on top of the stove.

"Now for the fun part!" Arely exclaimed. She handed me a large utensil with a flat surface and showed me how to lightly pound the *tostones* to flatten them like wafers. Then, we stuck the pan back into the oven to let them bake some more.

Ten minutes later, the three of us sat down with steaming mugs of tea and shared a plate full of crispy browned *tostones*. "This is such a special treat. Thank you!" I exclaimed. "I thought I was playing it safe by grabbing a banana from your fruit bowl earlier, but I'm glad it wasn't a banana after all. I think I'll be able to distinguish the two next time I'm at the grocery store, and I think I'll choose a bunch of plantains instead of bananas and see what I can make!"

Name _____ Date _____

4 What is the theme of this passage? How does Christina's point of view help convey this theme?

_____

_____

_____

_____

_____

Name _____ Date _____

Esperanza Rising

Answer Numbers 1 through 10 on your Answer Sheet. Base your answers on the novel *Esperanza Rising*.

1 The setting of the beginning of the novel is

   A. a farm in Los Angeles, California.

   B. a camp cabin in Arvin, California.

   C. a large ranch in Aguascalientes, Mexico.

   D. at the border between Mexico and the United States.

2 Who are the main characters in the novel?

   F. Isabel and Josephina

   G. Marisol and Abuelita

   H. Esperanza and Miguel

   I. Tío Luis and Tío Marco

3 When Esperanza and Miguel are described as being "on opposite sides of a deep river," it means

   A. Miguel is 16 years old and Esperanza is only 13 years old.

   B. Miguel is more privileged because he knows how to fix things on the ranch.

   C. Esperanza is wealthy and of a higher class than Miguel, who is a servant's son.

   D. Esperanza lives on a ranch on one side of the river and Miguel lives on the other side.

4 Which characters create an obstacle for Esperanza?

   F. Miguel and Marta

   G. Ramona and Abuelita

   H. Hortensia and Alfonso

   I. Tío Luis and Tío Marco

Name _____ Date _____

5 Which of the following sentences best describes the conflict Esperanza and her mother face?

   A. Abuelita unraveled all of Esperanza's crocheted rows and made her start over.

   B. Esperanza pricked her finger on the thorn of a rose, and Mama said it was bad luck.

   C. Esperanza's father died, and Esperanza and her mother must flee to the United States.

   D. Esperanza's father died, and she does not have the birthday party she would normally have had.

6 When Esperanza boards the train in Zacatecas, she is

   F. eager but shy.

   G. joyful and excited.

   H. hopeful but afraid.

   I. arrogant and rude.

7 Marta is an important minor character in the novel because she

   A. likes Miguel and wants to take him away from Esperanza.

   B. is an American citizen and looks down on Mexican nationals.

   C. blindly follows the strikers without thinking of the welfare of her own mother.

   D. forces Esperanza to think about the lives and conditions of all migrant families and not just her own.

8 After Esperanza's mother is hospitalized, Esperanza

   F. panics and asks Miguel to take her back to Aguascalientes to find Abuelita.

   G. joins Marta and the strikers to protest the low wages and squalor of the Mexican camps.

   H. realizes she must become *la patrona*, and must work to pay the bills and bring Abuelita to her mother.

   I. knows she must think of herself to survive and not worry about her mother who is cared for by doctors and nurses.

9 The climax, or turning point of the novel, occurs when

A. the immigration officials raid the camps and load strikers onto buses.

B. Esperanza gives Isabel the doll to console her when she did not win Queen of the May.

C. Miguel brings Abuelita to California and Tío Luis and Tío Marco no longer have control over their lives.

D. Esperanza argues with Miguel because he agreed to dig ditches instead of confronting his boss at the railroad.

10 A proverb is a familiar saying that is wise or contains a life lesson. Which of the following statements from the novel is NOT a proverb?

F. "Watch your fingers."

G. "There is no rose without thorns."

H. "He who falls today may rise tomorrow."

I. "Wait a little while and the fruit will fall into your hand."

Name _____ Date _____

Brian's Winter

Answer Numbers 1 through 10 on your Answer Sheet. Base your answers on the novel _Brian's Winter_.

1 Brian is alone in the Canadian wilderness because he

   A. went on a hike and got lost.

   B. wanted to run away from his family.

   C. was in a plane crash and was marooned there.

   D. was being tested on his survival skills by the Boy Scouts.

2 Brian is relieved when the food rations in the survival kit are gone because

   F. the food makes him think of home.

   G. he doesn't like the taste of the food.

   H. the food rations do not include meat.

   I. the freeze-dried food makes him sick.

3 Why is it best for Brian to boil meat in stew?

   A. Brian is afraid that flies will contaminate his food.

   B. Brian wants to make sure the meat is fully cooked.

   C. The nutrients from the meat will be retained in the broth.

   D. Boiling the meat in a stew will keep bears and wolves away.

4 What does Brian learn from observing the wolves?

   F. He learns to hunt.

   G. They run in packs.

   H. They are not afraid of him.

   I. They visit on a regular schedule.

5 Which of the following sentences does NOT support the idea that Brian is resourceful?

    A. He sews clothes of animal hides.

    B. He misses the important warnings that summer is ending.

    C. He uses the cord in his sleeping bag to string his heavy bow.

    D. He manages to seal and fortify the walls and doors of his shelter.

6 The migrating geese are an important sign for Brian, because it means

    F. he will not be able to hunt geese.

    G. winter is coming and he must prepare.

    H. summer is coming and more food will be available.

    I. more rainy weather is in store and it will be difficult to hunt.

7 After Betty sprays the bear, Brian is

    A. grateful to Betty for saving his life.

    B. hungry because he has no food left.

    C. angry because his shelter is damaged.

    D. making plans to hunt the bear with his bow and arrows.

8 How does Brian feel about both the moose and the deer?

    F. elated

    G. fearful

    H. indifferent

    I. remorseful

Name _____ Date _____

9 What effect do the snowshoes have on Brian's outlook?

    A. They enable him to stay at his camp more.

    B. They boost his confidence in making clothing.

    C. They give him more freedom outside the shelter.

    D. They give him something to work on during a cold winter's night.

10 By the end of the novel, Brian is

    F. eager to return home to his family.

    G. reluctant to leave the wilderness he has come to enjoy.

    H. eager to fly in a plane after such a long time in the wilderness.

    I. reluctant to leave the Smallhorns because they have become his family.

Tracking Trash: Flotsam, Jetsam, and the Science of Ocean Motion

Answer Numbers 1 through 10 on your Answer Sheet. Base your answers on the novel *Tracking Trash: Flotsam, Jetsam, and the Science of Ocean Motion*.

1 Which of the following statements is a fact?

   A. Franklin published the first map describing the so-called Gulf Stream in 1769.

   B. Dr. Ebbesmeyer's methods for understanding the ocean are, well, just a little unusual.

   C. Curt suspected that the toy-recovery pattern had something to do with the path the toys were following in the ocean.

   D. The warm waters of the Gulf Stream are believed to heat the winds that, in turn, carry a pleasant climate to northern Europe.

2 What initially caused a turn in Curt's career?

   F. His friend, Jim, showed him a computer program he had created.

   G. His mother showed him an article about the sneakers on beaches near Seattle.

   H. Captain Charles Moore found a floating patch of garbage and contacted Curt about it.

   I. Beachcombers contacted Curt about sneakers, toys, and hockey gloves they had found on beaches.

3 Which phrase summarizes the main idea of page 8?

   A. finding the location of the International Date Line

   B. how sailors use maps with grids on them to find their way

   C. how the ocean is divided into towns and streets, but has few landmarks

   D. finding the exact location of the *Hansa Carrier* at the time of the sneaker spill

Name _____ Date _____

④ With which of the following statements is the author trying to persuade the reader to agree?

   F. Beachcombers play a vital role in scientific research.

   G. The OSCURS program is an important scientific tool.

   H. We all need to stop using disposable plastics in order to protect our oceans.

   I. The Eastern Garbage Patch is where currents have brought plastic trash from different locations.

⑤ Which of the following statements is NOT evidence for the dangers of plastic in our environment?

   A. Plastic is one of the most indestructible materials on the planet.

   B. Plastic is eaten by marine life, such as sea turtles, jellyfish, and birds.

   C. Even the smallest pieces of plastic interact with contaminants in the ocean.

   D. Fish caught by commercial fishermen are contaminated when they eat contaminated jellyfish.

⑥ What evidence does the author give to support the statement that plastic is destroying one of Earth's most important natural resources?

   F. The author points out that plastic and contaminants can end up in our own food chain.

   G. Curt Ebbesmeyer thinks we cannot clean up the plastic in the Eastern Garbage Patch piece by piece.

   H. In 2005, Charlie and his team used a new type of trawl to analyze the amount of plastic below the sea's surface.

   I. The author explains that experiments that cannot be carried out in real life can be done with the OSCURS program.

Name _____ Date _____

7 Which of the following statements is an opinion?

   A. I think in our family of creatures we are misbehaving badly.

   B. Jim was a scientist at the National Oceanic and Atmospheric Administration.

   C. The *Hansa Carrier* was loaded to capacity when it collided with a vicious storm.

   D. OSCURS is a program that oceanographers use to fine-tune world surface current maps.

8 Ghost nets

   F. are predators in the ocean.

   G. are attached to fishing boats.

   H. help the environment by catching trash.

   I. endanger marine animals and destroy coral reefs.

9 Dr. Mary Donohue's viewpoint on ghost nets is

   A. neutral.

   B. positive.

   C. negative.

   D. unbiased.

10 The exact location of the Garbage Patch

   F. cannot be determined.

   G. changes from year to year.

   H. is found by beachcombers.

   I. is always in the same place.